JOHN QUINCY ADAMS

PRESIDENTIAL ✦ LEADERS

JOHN QUINCY ADAMS

DEBBIE LEVY

⌐ LERNER PUBLICATIONS COMPANY / MINNEAPOLIS

A NOTE ABOUT SPELLINGS: Most people of John Quincy Adams's era spelled words quite differently than we do today. They also used different grammar and capitalization. This book preserves the original spelling and punctuation of all historical writings.

Copyright © 2005 by Debbie Levy

All rights reserved. International copyright secured. No part of this book may be reproduced, stored in a retrieval system, or transmitted in any form or by any means—electronic, mechanical, photocopying, recording, or otherwise—without the prior written permission of Lerner Publications Company, except for the inclusion of brief quotations in an acknowledged review.

Lerner Publications Company
A division of Lerner Publishing Group
241 First Avenue North
Minneapolis, MN 55401 U.S.A.

Website address: www.lernerbooks.com

Library of Congress Cataloging-in-Publication Data

Levy, Debbie.
    John Quincy Adams / by Debbie Levy.
        p.   cm. — (Presidential leaders)
    Includes bibliographical references and index.
    Contents: Child of the revolution—A boy in Europe—Teenage diplomat—A rocky start—Carving out a career—Politics and advancement—Man of the world—Seasoned secretary of state—A disappointing presidency begins—From bad to worse—Old man eloquent.
    ISBN: 0–8225–0825–7 (lib. bdg. : alk. paper)
    1. Adams, John Quincy, 1767–1848—Juvenile literature. 2. Presidents—United States—Biography—Juvenile literature. [1. Adams, John Quincy, 1767–1848. 2. Presidents.]
I. Title. II. Series.
E377.L46 2005
973.5'5'092—dc22   2003025397

Manufactured in the United States of America
1 2 3 4 5 6 – JR – 10 09 08 07 06 05

CONTENTS

———— ✧ ————

John Quincy Adams is the only person to be elected to the House of Representatives after being U.S. president. As a representative, he remained outspoken about his beliefs until the end of his life.

INTRODUCTION

[W]hat can I, upon the verge of my seventy-fourth birthday, with a shaking hand, a darkening eye, a drowsy brain . . . what can I do for the cause of God and Man? for the progress of human emancipation [freedom]? for the suppression [stopping] of the African Slave-trade?
—diary entry of former president and congressman John Quincy Adams, May 29, 1841

It was Monday, January 25, 1842, in the U.S. House of Representatives. On Mondays, congressmen could present petitions, or formal requests, sent to them by the nation's citizens. As usual, the elderly congressman from Massachusetts had some petitions to read. As usual, some of these petitions protested the existence of slavery in the southern states. And, as usual, the congressman was not allowed to present these antislavery petitions.

Congressman John Quincy Adams was barred from presenting his antislavery petitions because back in 1836 Congress had passed a resolution, or decision, known as the "gag rule." This rule specifically banned congressmen from presenting citizens' petitions about slavery. Representatives of the slaveholding southern states did not want Congress to debate slavery. They insisted that slavery was central to the southern way of life and that antislavery northerners such as Adams did not understand it.

The idea that Congress could stop citizens from petitioning their government and using their right to free speech set Adams on edge. And the arguments that some southern slaveholders made to justify slavery practically pushed him over that edge. So on this particular Monday, Congressman Adams presented an outrageous petition from the citizens of Haverhill, Massachusetts. It asked that the U.S. Congress "immediately adopt measures to dissolve [end] the Union of these States." In other words, the petition asked that the United States of America be broken apart.

Adams's fellow congressmen seemed stunned. One congressman asked the Speaker of the House (who is in charge of the proceedings), "Is it in order to move to burn the petition in the presence of the House?" Then another congressman proposed that Adams should be censured, or officially reprimanded. Adams exclaimed, "Good!"

By this time, Congressman Adams was also an ex-president of the United States, an ex-secretary of state, an ex-ambassador to four countries, and an ex-U.S. senator. He did not really want to dissolve the nation that he had served for a lifetime. He simply wanted a chance to debate slavery. The possible censure gave him the perfect opportunity. Adams knew the rules of the House of Representatives. He had a right to defend himself against the accusations in a censure resolution, and he could say anything he wanted in his defense. With his outrageous petition, Adams gained for himself the right to speak about slavery despite the gag rule for as long as he liked.

Over the next two weeks, Adams practically took over proceedings in the House of Representatives with his "defense" against the censure resolution. His defense was an all-out attack on his accusers and the slaveholding southern states. The excited, even frenzied, former president called his opponents "beef-witted blunderhead[s]" and "drunk with whiskey and drunk with slavery." He said that slave-holding southerners and their representatives in Congress were guilty of crushing the freedoms on which the nation was founded.

Finally, an exhausted Adams finished his speechmaking. He allowed the censure resolution to come to a vote. The House of Representatives defeated it on February 4, 1842. Adams was not censured. As if itself exhausted by the ordeal, the gag rule gradually lost support. On December 3, 1844, Congress voted to overturn it.

Four years later, the outspoken John Quincy Adams was dead. This man who knew and worked with the Founding Fathers had done what they never did: he publicly criticized slavery and stood up for freedom for all. His passionate opposition to slavery capped an extraordinary public life, showing the strength of his convictions and the depth of his love for his country.

CHAPTER ONE

CHILD OF THE REVOLUTION

*I make but a poor figure at composition, my
head is much too fickle, my thoughts are
running after birds eggs, play and trifles
[unimportant things], till I get vexed with
myself. Mamma has a troublesome task to keep
me steady, and I own I am ashamed of myself.*

—letter from John Quincy Adams to his father,
John Adams, June 2, 1777

When John Quincy Adams was born on July 11, 1767, in
a village outside of Boston, Massachusetts, called Braintree,
his parents began fretting about his future almost immediately. John Adams, a busy Massachusetts lawyer, worried
about college for his infant son. Abigail Adams worried
about his health. But health was only the beginning of
Abigail's worries. To Abigail, Johnny and his older sister
Nabby were like little "plants." They had to be "raised and
cultivated" to spread "virtue and happiness through the

Abigail and John Adams were very involved in their children's lives and encouraged a rigorous schedule of learning in a wide variety of subjects.

───────────────── ✧ ─────────────────

human race." Both parents wanted their son to grow up to be—in a word—great.

With such concerns in mind, Johnny's parents bombarded him with academic lessons, moral teachings, and warnings. They told him he could become "great and manly," as his father wrote in a letter, so long as he fixed his "attention upon great and glorious objects" and tried to "weed out every meanness."

Much of the work of raising and cultivating Johnny, Nabby, and the two brothers born after them, Charles and Thomas, fell to Abigail Adams. John's legal career often took him away from the family's farm in Braintree and their townhouse in Boston. Abigail was certainly up to the task. Like nearly all women of her time, she did not attend school. But she was intelligent and widely read, and she held strong opinions on everything from child rearing to politics.

The worrying and warnings seemed to pay off. Johnny was a well-behaved boy who learned arithmetic, reading, and writing and took up the study of Latin and Greek at a very young age. He seemed to love learning, but he also seemed anxious to please his parents. When he was seven years old, he wrote to his father:

> *I hope I grow a better Boy and that you will have no occasion to be ashamed of me when you return. Mr. Thaxter [Johnny's tutor] says I learn my Books well—he is a very good Master. I read my Books to Mamma. We all long to see you; I am Sir your Dutiful Son,*
>
> *John Quincy Adams*

FAMILY OF PATRIOTS

By 1774, when Johnny was seven, Boston and its surrounding areas were tense places to live. Great Britain still ruled its American colonies, and many residents of the Massachusetts Bay colony objected strongly to British rule. Braintree was home to many patriots, people who opposed British rule. The Adams family fell squarely in the patriot camp, and Johnny's father was a leader of the patriots.

In 1774 the people of Massachusetts selected John Adams to represent them in the Continental Congress taking place that autumn in Philadelphia, Pennsylvania.

Delegates (representatives) from the colonies met to discuss their complaints against Great Britain. Johnny stayed home with his mother and siblings, while John Adams became a leading member of the Congress.

Philadelphia was three hundred miles from Braintree, a distance that took two weeks to travel by stagecoach. Johnny saw less and less of his father but awaited his letters eagerly. The young boy frequently rode ten miles on horseback to pick up the mail and other things his mother needed in Boston.

WAR HITS HOME

In April 1775, tension between American colonists and British troops exploded into war. The first battles of the American Revolution took places in the Massachusetts towns of Lexington and Concord, twenty miles from Braintree. After the fighting, the American militiamen (volunteer soldiers) returned to their farms and homes, and the British soldiers went back to their headquarters in Boston. Still, tension continued to increase.

Soon violence broke out again. On June 17, 1775, the people of Braintree awoke to the sound of cannon fire. The booming noise was the Battle of Bunker Hill, raging only a few miles away in the village of Charlestown. Rather than take cover, Johnny and his mother climbed a nearby hill for a better view of the fighting. All they could see was smoke from the cannons and guns.

The Americans surrendered at the Battle of Bunker Hill but suffered few deaths. The British, although they won the hilly battleground, suffered many deaths. By the following spring of 1776, continual attacks by American militiamen drove the British out of Boston altogether.

Not content merely to take cover when the Battle of Bunker Hill began, Abigail and Johnny climbed atop a hill to better view the battle. Some like-minded citizens climbed atop their roofs to take in the whole scene.

————————————— ✧ —————————————

Although war no longer raged in the Adamses' backyard, the struggle to throw off British rule was still very much a part of their lives. In 1776 John Adams and other members of the Continental Congress signed their names to the Declaration of Independence. Adams had helped shape this important document, along with others such as Benjamin Franklin from Philadelphia and Thomas Jefferson of Virginia, the main author. The declaration announced the formation of a new and independent nation known as the United States of America. Those who signed it were considered traitors to Britain's King George III. Johnny was afraid his father might be killed for disloyalty to the king.

Johnny continued his education as best he could during the war. He did not attend formal schools but instead received instruction from a tutor. Classes had been disrupted by the war. And besides, Johnny's mother feared he would be exposed to bad influences in the local school. His father agreed. He wrote to Abigail that she should tell Johnny "to keep himself out of the Company of rude children."

Johnny seemed unlikely to join up with the wrong crowd. "I wish, Sir, you would give me some instructions, with regard to my time, & advise me how to proportion my Studies & my Play, in writing, & I will keep them by me, & endeavour [try] to follow them," he wrote to his father in the summer of 1777. John Adams wrote back with ambitious suggestions for his son. Among these was the idea that ten-year-old Johnny should master the writings of the ancient Greek historian Thucydides, "of whom I hope you will make yourself perfect Master, in original Language, which is Greek, the most perfect of all human Languages."

PLANNING A JOURNEY

But before Johnny could travel back through ancient history, he set out on a different journey. At the end of 1777, the Continental Congress asked John Adams to travel to Paris, France, as soon as possible. Congress wanted Johnny's father to try to convince the French government to support the American Revolution. (The famous patriot, printer, and scientist Benjamin Franklin was already there on the same mission.) This was an important and dangerous assignment. Crossing the Atlantic Ocean from Boston in winter was rarely attempted because the stormy winter seas could be very dangerous. Crossing during wartime raised additional dangers, since British ship captains were likely to attack a U.S. ship.

Despite the dangers, John Adams not only accepted the assignment—he also decided to take Johnny with him. Johnny was eager for the adventure, and Abigail agreed that the voyage would be good for her son. He would spend time with his father, learn French, and see part of Europe.

Just as important, as Johnny's tutor John Thaxter noted, he would be "laying the foundations of a great man." That after all, had been the plan for John Quincy Adams from the very start.

CHAPTER TWO

A BOY IN EUROPE

One more storm would very probably [have] carried us to the bottom of the sea.

—letter from twelve-year-old John Quincy Adams to his mother, describing the leaky ship in which he made his third trip across the Atlantic Ocean in less than two years

The weeks leading up to the journey to Europe were busy with preparations. The Adamses kept their voyage secret so British spies would not try to stop it. To preserve secrecy, Johnny and his father boarded their ship, the *Boston,* under cover of darkness on February 13, 1778.

At first, the journey was uneventful. The food was bad, and the ship was smelly and dirty. But Johnny busied himself by learning French from another passenger. Soon the ship was tailed by British ships but managed to escape them. Next, the weather took a terrible turn. For three days, the *Boston* was rocked by a violent thunderstorm. Lightning struck the main mast, injuring crew members.

One was burned so badly that he died, after days of extreme suffering.

A small ship offered no place to hide from the danger and frightful sights. "To describe the Ocean, the Waves, the Winds, the Ship, her Motions, Rollings, Wringings and Agonies . . . is impossible," John Adams wrote in his diary. Johnny, like his father and nearly everyone else, was seasick. But he held up as well as the adults. After the storm passed,

———————————— ✧ ————————————

Traveling to Europe in the 1700s was full of risks. The journey was long, with storms to weather and British ships to avoid. If tragedy struck, passengers would have to abandon ship like the men below, who are lowering themselves into a lifeboat.

John Adams recorded proudly in his diary: "Mr. Johnny's Behaviour gave me a Satisfaction that I cannot express—fully sensible of our Danger, he was constantly endeavouring to bear it with a manly Patience, very attentive to me and his Thoughts constantly running in a serious Strain."

The skies cleared, and the *Boston* sailed on. The ship's captain, apparently impressed by Johnny's calmness during the storm, taught him to use a sailing tool called a mariner's compass and explained the workings of the ship's many sails. Another adventure arose when the *Boston* came across an armed British commercial ship and exchanged cannon fire with it. The Americans quickly overpowered the British ship and brought its crew and captain on board as prisoners.

A TASTE OF FRANCE

Finally, on Monday, March 30, 1778, the *Boston* entered the harbor at Bordeaux, France. The voyage of three thousand miles had taken six weeks. Johnny and his father were in Europe for the first time in their lives. They enjoyed Bordeaux—especially the food, after six weeks aboard the *Boston*.

After resting for several days, Johnny and John Adams traveled five hundred miles by coach to the French capital of Paris. They moved in with Benjamin Franklin in his home in the suburb of Passy.

Johnny, who was not quite eleven years old, enrolled in a private boarding school in Passy. His day started at six in the morning with two hours of classes, followed by an hour for breakfast and play. He attended more classes from nine in the morning to noon, two to four thirty, and five to seven thirty at night. The students went to bed at nine.

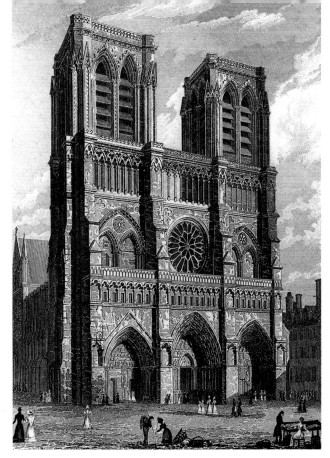

Built between 1163 and 1250, Notre Dame Cathedral in Paris, France, is a stunning example of Gothic architecture and remains one of the most famous sights in Europe, just as when Johnny visited it in 1778.

Johnny's time was not all spent in studies. He saw the famous sights of Paris and its surroundings, including the Palace of Versailles and Notre Dame Cathedral. Most of all, he loved attending the theater, concerts, and operas. Braintree and Boston had offered nothing like the cultural attractions Johnny found in Europe.

AT SEA AGAIN

John Adams proposed to Congress that only one representative from the United States was needed in France. In

February 1779, John Adams learned that Congress had decided to appoint Benjamin Franklin as the sole U.S. minister (ambassador) to France. Father and son set sail in June 1779 on a French ship, the *Sensible.* On board the ship was France's new minister to the United States, the Chevalier de La Luzerne. Showing a knack for getting along with his elders, Johnny struck up a friendship with the French diplomat. He gave English lessons to the ambassador and his secretary. Both men were impressed with this boy, who seemed ahead of his years. "The Ambassador said he was astonished at my son's knowledge," wrote John Adams, "that he was a master of his own language like a professor."

On August 2, 1779, a crew member from the *Sensible* rowed John and Johnny to the shores of Braintree, where they were met by—nobody. No word had reached Abigail of her husband and son's voyage, and she was completely surprised and delighted by their return. The family spent the rest of the summer and early fall together. Soon the new nation called on Johnny's father once again. In October 1779, John Adams learned that Congress had appointed him to return to France. This time he was to go as a minister with powers to negotiate treaties of peace and trade with Great Britain. The war with Britain was not over, but Adams was to wait in Europe until the time was right.

And so three months after crossing the ocean between Europe and the United States, a group of Adamses set out to do it again. Abigail still stayed home, but she and John decided that it was time for nine-year-old Charles Adams to venture abroad. Johnny wanted to stay home. He was twelve years old, and in a few years, he would be old enough to attend Harvard College. He wanted to study at highly respected Andover Academy to prepare.

Abigail and John disagreed, and they turned Johnny's opinion around. In a farewell letter to her son, Abigail explained that his experiences out in the world would form in him "the Character of the Hero and the Statesman." She added, "It is not in the still calm of life . . . that great characters are formed. . . . The Habits of a vigorous mind are formed in contending [dealing] with difficulties."

A EUROPEAN EDUCATION

John, Johnny, and Charles reached Paris on February 9, 1780. The very next day, Johnny was back in boarding school in Passy, this time accompanied by his brother. Although the younger boy was terribly homesick, Johnny dove back into his studies. In a letter to his father in March, he described his daily work schedule. It included everything from Latin, Greek, geometry, and fractions to writing, drawing, and geography. Seeking nearly always to gain his father's advice and approval, he concluded, "As a young boy can not apply himself to all those Things and keep a remembrance of them all I should desire that you would let me know what of those I must begin upon at first. I am your Dutiful Son, John Quincy Adams."

Johnny's father wrote back immediately, telling him to focus most on Greek and Latin, and least on writing and drawing. He added: "P.S.: The next Time you write to me, I hope you will take more care to write well. Cant you keep a steadier hand?"

Soon the Adamses were on the move again. In July 1780, John Adams's diplomatic work took him to the city of Amsterdam, in Holland (also called the Netherlands). There, Johnny and Charles studied with private tutors at the University of Leyden. Among other things, Johnny learned to read and speak the Dutch language.

By January 1781, Johnny had so advanced in his studies that the University of Leyden admitted him as a student. The thirteen-year-old enjoyed the intellectual atmosphere of the university. Before he turned fourteen, however, he was on the move again—on a voyage to the capital of Russia, Saint Petersburg.

Young Johnny relished his travels abroad and kept detailed records of them in his diary. As much as he had enjoyed Paris, Johnny wrote that Saint Petersburg, Russia, was a far superior city.

CHAPTER THREE

TEENAGE DIPLOMAT

Meanwhile I send you a Son who is the greatest Traveller of his age, and . . . I think as promising and manly a youth as is in the whole World.

—letter from John Adams to Abigail Adams,
describing their seventeen-year-old son
John Quincy Adams, 1784

Johnny's ability to speak French and get along with adults led him to Russia. In the summer of 1781, Francis Dana, a young lawyer serving as secretary to John Adams, learned that Congress had given him a new assignment. Dana was to go to Russia and ask the Russian empress, Catherine the Great, to recognize the government of the United States as an independent nation. The official language of the Russian court (the royal government) was not Russian but French. Dana did not speak French. Johnny Adams did.

Few Americans, young or old, traveled to distant Russia. On July 7, 1781, four days before his fourteenth

birthday, Johnny set out with
Dana in a new carriage bound
for Saint Petersburg.

The trip was long and eye-
opening. Along their route, the
travelers visited Berlin, the capital
of Prussia (part of modern
Germany). Berlin, Johnny wrote,
was "the handsomest and most
regular city I ever saw." He did
not find all the sights he encoun-
tered so agreeable. In the coun-
tryside, he wrote to his father,
"All the Farmers are in the most
abject [miserable] slavery, they

Francis Dana

——————— ✧ ———————

are bought and sold like so many beasts, and are sometimes
even chang'd [traded] for dogs or horses."

Johnny and Dana reached Saint Petersburg at the end
of August. This, Johnny wrote, was truly the most beautiful
city of all. But both the boy and his employer experienced
frustrations in Russia. Dana's diplomatic work and Johnny's
services as translator and secretary came to a quick stand-
still. Empress Catherine declined to recognize the new
United States of America. That left neither Dana nor
Johnny with much official business to conduct.

ON HIS OWN

Turning to his studies, Johnny could find no suitable
school or tutor. He explained to his father: "There is
nobody here but Princes and Slaves. The Slaves cannot have
their children instructed, and the nobility that chuse to

have their's send them into foreign countries. There is not one school to be found in the whole city." Johnny spent his time learning German on his own, practicing French, Latin, and Greek, and reading English books he found at a library. His time in Saint Petersburg was not entirely unpleasant. He loved to browse bookstores and began a lifelong habit of collecting books. He also took walks, met people, and experienced a Russian winter—far longer and harsher than winters at home.

Rather than stay for a second winter in Saint Petersburg, Johnny decided to leave. He was concerned about falling behind in his studies. His parents and Francis Dana agreed that he should return to his father in Holland, where he could study and work as John Adams's secretary.

A LEISURELY TOUR

Johnny did not exactly hurry back to Holland. His travel was slowed by winter weather but also by the sheer fun he found in visiting new places. He left Saint Petersburg on October 30, 1782, taking three weeks to reach Stockholm, Sweden. Although only fifteen, Johnny had grown used to making himself at home in new places. In the Swedish capital, he blended into adult society. People invited him to dinners and balls, which he attended happily. He found Stockholm such a friendly place that he stayed for more than a month.

More hospitality greeted Johnny as he made his way across northern Europe. Seemingly older than his years, he impressed people wherever he went. Part of his attraction was simply that he was a citizen of the United States, the world's newest nation. Johnny also charmed people with his intelligence and conversation. He enjoyed talking with businesspeople, leading citizens, intellectuals, and women. He even looked older than his years. His hairline was starting to recede, and he had reached his adult height of five feet seven inches, with a stocky build.

As Johnny spent the winter months on his own, back in Holland his father wondered where he was. When Johnny finally showed up in the spring of 1783, John Adams found that the boy who had gone off to Russia had come home an adult. He wrote to Abigail of their son, "He is grown a Man in Understanding as well as Stature."

FAMILY REUNION

While Johnny was in Russia, his father had been negotiating a peace treaty with Great Britain. The work was not yet finished, so Johnny and his father returned to Paris, where the peace talks were being held. Johnny—who had begun referring to himself as "JQA"—helped prepare the necessary paperwork. In the final treaty, Great Britain recognized the United States as an independent nation. Known as the Treaty of Paris, it was signed on September 3, 1783.

In the months following the signing of the Treaty of Paris, the older and younger Adams men spent time in France, Britain, and Holland. John Adams had diplomatic assignments. JQA returned to his studies so that he would be prepared to attend Harvard. He also found plenty of time for his favorite pastime, attending the theater, as well as for visiting art galleries, libraries, and bookshops.

When John Adams learned that Congress wanted him to continue his diplomatic work in Europe, he sent for his wife, Abigail, to join him. Abigail arranged for the two younger Adams boys, Charles and Thomas, to stay at home with relatives. She and JQA's older sister, Nabby, sailed across the Atlantic in the summer of 1784. They arrived in London on July 21, and JQA was there to greet them.

When he left Massachusetts in 1779, JQA had been twelve years old. He was seventeen, and his mother had not seen him for five years. She could hardly recognize him. As Abigail wrote to her sister of the reunion: "I drew back not really believing my Eyes—till he cried out, Oh my Mamma! and my dear Sister. Nothing but the Eyes at first appeared what he once was. His appearance is that of a Man."

The reunited family traveled to Paris, where John Adams joined Thomas Jefferson and Benjamin Franklin to negotiate more treaties with European nations. They rented a house in Auteuil, a suburb in the hills outside the city. JQA worked on his studies in the mornings and again after a family dinner at two o'clock. Thomas Jefferson visited frequently. The teenager and the author of the Declaration of Independence discussed books, science, art, and history. "I love to be with [Jefferson]," JQA wrote, "because he is a man of very extensive learning and pleasing manners." JQA also enjoyed spending time with the European intellectuals whom he met in Paris.

GOING HOME

In April 1785, after nine months in Auteuil, John Adams learned that Congress had appointed him to serve as U.S. minister to Britain. For JQA, it was time to make a decision. Should he go to London with his parents, or should he finally go home? John and Abigail Adams believed their son should return to Massachusetts and follow in John's footsteps. He would attend Harvard College and then prepare for a career as a lawyer.

His Mother's Son

By the time he was fourteen, John Quincy Adams was treated by the world as if he were an adult. To his mother, however, he was always a son—someone to be corrected, instructed, and fussed at, even long after his childhood ended.

Abigail Adams was full of advice about how her Johnny might improve himself, no matter how far away he was. When her boy was in Paris in 1780, she wrote him, "You must consider that every Moment of your time is precious, if trifled away never to be recalled. Do not spend too much of it in recreation . . . and whatever you undertake aim to make yourself perfect in it, for if it is worth doing at all, it is worth doing well."

When John Adams took Johnny to Holland later in 1780, Abigail was concerned about the move. Still, she thought Johnny might get something out of it. As she wrote her son, he should try to adopt the "universal neatness and Cleanliness" of the people of Holland, which hopefully "will cure you of all your slovenly tricks, and that you will learn from them industry, economy and frugality."

Nearly twenty-five years later, when Adams was a U.S. senator, his mother was still working on improving him. "Now I hope you never appear in Senate with a beard two days old, or otherwise make what is called a shabby appearance," she wrote to him. "I do not wish a Senator to . . . give occasion to the world to ask what kind of mother he had?"

——————— ◇

This statue in Quincy, Massachusetts, depicts JQA and his mother, Abigail.

JQA agreed but had doubts. In his diary entry of April 26, 1785, he wrote, "After having been traveling for these seven years almost all over Europe . . . to return to spend one or two years in . . . College, subjected to all the rules which I have so long been freed from; then to plunge into the dry and tedious study of the Law for three years . . . It is really a prospect somewhat discouraging for a youth of my ambition."

Despite his hesitations, JQA left Europe for the United States the next month. The experienced traveler had his eighteenth birthday aboard ship a week before he arrived in New York Harbor.

CHAPTER FOUR

A ROCKY START

I felt a depression of spirits to which I have thitherto [until now] been entirely a stranger.
—John Quincy Adams, diary entry, 1787

New York City was the capital of the United States in July 1785 and a center of the nation's political and social life. When JQA came ashore, he immediately began a round of socializing. Because of his travels, everyone wanted to talk with him. He stayed with Richard Henry Lee, then the president of Congress. (The nation's government was organized under a set of agreements among the thirteen states known as the Articles of Confederation—not yet the Constitution. There was no president of the United States.) He discussed government affairs with congressmen, diplomats from foreign countries, and other important New Yorkers. It was a whirlwind homecoming.

But JQA was not really home yet. After a month in New York, he headed on horseback for Massachusetts. At the end of August, JQA was back in his hometown of Braintree, where he reunited with family and friends.

He did not expect to stay in Braintree for long. The plan was to enroll in Harvard, located in Cambridge, on the Charles River opposite Boston. Seeking to receive credit for his studies in Europe, JQA wished to enter Harvard as a junior, or third-year student. But all did not go according to plan. Although he impressed people everywhere he went, JQA did not properly impress Harvard when he traveled to Cambridge for his college admissions test. The college would not admit Johnny as an upperclassman until he improved his Greek and Latin.

The rejection was a blow to the young man. Instead of packing off to Cambridge, in September 1785, he began six months of private study with one of his uncles in the Massachusetts town of Haverhill. In March 1786, JQA went to Cambridge again to be tested by the Harvard faculty. This time, they decided he was prepared enough to join the junior class.

COLLEGE STUDENT

At Harvard, JQA enjoyed his classes, especially math and astronomy. Algebra, he wrote, was "as entertaining as it is useful." He learned to play the flute. He socialized with other students and with the young women of Cambridge, sometimes staying out until four in the morning.

But JQA worked as much as he socialized. His nearby relatives were concerned that he studied too hard and might become sick. He joined with like-minded students in a literary club and in the academic honor society, Phi Beta Kappa.

Established in 1636, Harvard has educated several presidents. JQA was the second Adams to enroll there. His father had graduated from Harvard in 1755.

Yet JQA was also harshly critical of others, both professors and students. He felt he knew more than many of them. Abigail warned him in a letter from London, "If you are conscious to yourself that you possess more knowledge upon some subjects than others of your standing, reflect that you have had greater opportunities of seeing the world. . . . How unpardonable would it have been in you to have been a blockhead."

What Abigail Adams may not have known was that JQA was as hard on himself as he was on others. He scolded himself in his diary for wasting his time and not accomplishing enough in his studies. He did tend to stray from his schoolwork on occasion and was known to oversleep and miss classes from time to time. These lapses in studiousness may not have made him much different from most students. But JQA—perhaps hearing his parents' urgings in his ears—always wanted to be better. Usually, he was. When he graduated in the summer of 1787, JQA ranked second out of a class of fifty-one students.

UNHAPPY BEGINNING

JQA knew from the time he entered college that his education was pointing him in one direction: toward the study of law. In those days, law students in the United States did not attend formal law schools. Instead, they studied, or "read law," with established lawyers who were willing to take them on as apprentices (lawyers in training).

JQA had never openly questioned the career choice that his parents—and everyone else—assumed would be his destiny. Yet JQA had no interest in being a lawyer. He yearned to become a scholar or a writer of great literary works. But those were not the paths that lay before him. JQA was dreading his future.

In the fall of 1787, JQA went to the town of Newburyport to begin his apprenticeship with Theophilus Parsons, a well-known Massachusetts lawyer. The experience was as miserable as he feared. Uninspired by legal studies and by the prospects of a life in the law, JQA was more than dissatisfied. He became extremely depressed. To escape his unhappiness, he often went on what he called "frolicks." During these times, he drank late into the night until he became, as he wrote in his diary, "Unfit for almost everything." He suffered headaches and dizziness and was constantly ill with colds or an upset stomach. He also had trouble sleeping.

In the fall of 1788, JQA was so depressed he could not continue his studies. John and Abigail Adams were back in the United States. In November 1788, John was elected the nation's first vice president under the newly adopted Constitution. (George Washington was elected president.) While his busy parents moved to the nation's capital in New York, the suffering JQA left Newburyport to stay with his Aunt Elizabeth Shaw in Haverhill. No medical treatments existed for the illness that modern doctors refer to as clinical depression and that JQA struggled with from this time throughout his adult life. Aunt Elizabeth cared for her nephew with homemade teas and similar remedies.

JQA returned to Newburyport in the spring of 1789. He began a romance with a beautiful fifteen-year-old named Mary Frazier. Before long, the couple was talking of marriage. Being with Mary improved JQA's spirits greatly. But as the relationship grew more serious, JQA's parents—particularly Abigail—worried about the dangers of marrying too early. Their opinions influenced the young man, who seemed nearly incapable of disappointing his parents. By the end of 1790, JQA and Mary broke off their relationship. Once again, JQA fell into depression's depths.

RELUCTANT LAWYER

In the meantime, JQA had completed his apprenticeship and set up a law office in Boston. His frame of mind did not promote success. He lost his first court case. He lacked energy to build a thriving legal practice. A diary entry revealed his condition: "All day at court. Dull. Anxious. Heavy. The present a deadly calm, and the future a chilling mist."

By then, John and Abigail Adams were living in Philadelphia, Pennsylvania. The U.S. Congress had moved the nation's capital to that city for a period of ten years. In 1800 it would relocate permanently to Washington, D.C. Concerned about JQA, John and Abigail urged him to visit them.

JQA accepted his parents' invitation in early 1791. While in Philadelphia, he dined with President and Mrs. Washington and visited Congress and the Supreme Court. The trip did not cure him of his depression, but his visit to the seat of government sparked JQA's interest in politics. His life began to take a new and less unhappy turn.

STEPPING INTO POLITICS

Before he visited Philadelphia, JQA had not taken part in politics and had declared himself uninterested in it. But after his return to Boston, he began to enter into political discussions with other lawyers. He also wrote articles, published in the *Boston Chronicle,* that defended the views of his father and of the Washington administration from attacks by others.

The nation was gradually dividing into two political parties, the Federalists and the Republicans (later known as the Democratic-Republicans). JQA followed the lead of his father and others in the new Federalist Party, including President Washington. Like these men, JQA supported a government with a strong central, or federal, government that would unify the nation.

JQA's writings brought him to the attention of influential people in politics. Federalists, of course, liked what JQA was saying. On the other side, Republicans disagreed with his arguments. They wanted the states to have more power than the federal government. Among their leaders was Thomas Jefferson—once JQA's hero but someone increasingly at odds with Vice President Adams and his son.

JQA enjoyed the attention his articles drew. He felt better and became more active in local politics. When the citizens of the north part of Braintree asked him to write legislation to transform them into a separate town, he took the assignment. The town's name was changed to Quincy, in honor of JQA's great-grandfather John Quincy.

His writing success inspired JQA to contemplate a life of writing. A quiet, bookish life had appealed to him for some time. But such a life did not seem to be his fate. In May 1794, JQA received a letter from his father informing him that President Washington had appointed JQA U.S. minister to the Netherlands. Vice President John Adams may well have praised his son to the president. But George Washington was himself familiar with JQA's vigorous newspaper defenses of his policies and probably wanted to reward his young supporter.

JQA's parents and friends were thrilled at his appointment. Becoming a diplomat at the age of twenty-six was a notable achievement. The annual salary of $4,500, far more than JQA had been able to earn as a lawyer, was also notable.

It seemed the only person who was not happy about the news was JQA. "I wish I could have been consulted before it [the nomination] was . . . made," he wrote in his diary in early June 1794. "I rather wish it had not been made at all." He feared he was not ready for the prominent position of being the nation's representative in a foreign country. He also mourned a life of duties that he assumed would be boring. Perhaps most importantly, he did not like the impression that he had obtained this desirable diplomatic job through his father's interference.

Yet John Quincy Adams did not fight his fate. His sense of duty to his country and his parents surely influenced him, as did his desire to make a career in a field other than the law. JQA may also have been attracted, privately, to the prestige of the position of a statesman. Whatever the true reasons, he packed his things and traveled to Philadelphia to accept his appointment. A new career was beginning.

CHAPTER FIVE

CARVING OUT A CAREER

I give it as my decided opinion, that Mr. Adams is the most valuable public character we have abroad, and that there remains no doubt in my mind that he will prove himself to be the ablest of our diplomatic corps [group].

—letter from President George Washington to Vice President John Adams, concerning the vice president's son, John Quincy Adams, February 20, 1797

On July 11, 1794, his twenty-seventh birthday, John Quincy Adams received his formal assignment as minister to the Netherlands from U.S. secretary of state Edmund Randolph. While in Philadelphia, Adams met with his brother Thomas and convinced him to come to Europe as his secretary. Thomas agreed, and on September 17, they sailed from Boston. They arrived at The Hague, the Netherlands' seat of government, in late October.

Though Amsterdam is the capital of the Netherlands, its seat
of government is The Hague (above), where many international
peace treaties have been signed through the years.

Soon after Adams took his post as minister, the French army overran the Netherlands in an attempt to control European countries bordering France. The invasion was part of the violent French Revolution, which had begun several years earlier. Suddenly, The Hague was occupied and run by French officers. Since Adams spoke French fluently, as well as Dutch, the invasion did not interfere with his work. His main duties were to keep the U.S. government informed of events in Europe and to have contact with the changing government of the Netherlands. These were jobs he found both stimulating and rewarding. Adams was in touch with French officials, Dutch citizens, and other diplomats to gather information. He wrote detailed reports of his findings, which he sent back home to Secretary of State Randolph.

As negative as Adams had been about becoming minister, he shone in the position. Randolph praised Adams's letters. This cheered Adams greatly. He felt as if his activities mattered to his country. He also enjoyed the company of other diplomats, with whom he took walks and had chats.

LOVE AND OTHER CHANGES

Under orders from the secretary of state, Adams traveled to London for an extended stay in late 1795. He was there to conduct treaty business with British officials, but he spent much of his time on personal affairs—in particular, on romance. While visiting with the family of Joshua Johnson, a U.S. official living in London, he met Johnson's seven daughters. Of the three Johnson daughters of marriageable age, he became interested in the middle one, twenty-one-year-old Louisa Catherine.

————— ✧

Adams found himself quite drawn to Louisa Johnson, who was well read, fluent in French, and a talented harp player.

John and Louisa spent a great deal of time together during his seven months in London. Like Adams, Louisa was fluent in French. She was smart, enjoyed music, liked to write poetry, and was considered quite beautiful.

Louisa was also more independent and outspoken than some young women of the time. And so she spoke up in the spring of 1796, when Adams proposed marriage—but not a marriage date. Louisa pressed him to be specific. He would not. Despite his marriage proposal, Adams seemed uncertain about the idea of actually getting married.

A new twist complicated Adams's uncertainty even more. Shortly after he returned to the Netherlands, he learned that President Washington had appointed him minister to Portugal. This new appointment was a promotion. In Portugal, Adams would be minister "plenipotentiary," meaning he would have full power to act for the U.S. government. This higher position gave him greater status and salary than he had in the Netherlands.

For Adams, who still hesitated to follow through on his marriage proposal, the appointment seemed a good opportunity to put off the marriage. He would perform his service in Portugal, and then he and Louisa could marry and return to the United States. Louisa had a different idea. Her fiancé could come to London on the way to Portugal, they would marry, and then go to Portugal together. This difference of opinion led to bitter arguments between the couple.

Finally, Adams changed his mind. He agreed to do what Louisa wanted. Adams and his brother Thomas, who was still his secretary, packed their things and crossed the English Channel. When he arrived in London in early July 1797, he learned of yet another complication. His father had been elected president the previous fall when George Washington declined to serve for a third term. President Adams had a new job for his son. He appointed the younger Adams minister plenipotentiary to Prussia. He would be going to the Prussian capital, the city of Berlin.

John Quincy Adams did not rejoice at this change. He had been assured that President Washington had named him minister to Portugal without interference from his father. He feared people would think he obtained this new position just because his father had become president.

And yet, as he had done three years before when he accepted his appointment to the Netherlands, Adams went forward with the new plan. He and Louisa were married on July 26, 1797. The bride was twenty-two years old. The groom had just had his thirtieth birthday.

LIFE IN PRUSSIA

Mr. and Mrs. John Quincy Adams left London for Prussia in October 1797. Thomas Adams traveled with them to continue as his brother's secretary. In early November, they arrived at the gates of Berlin. There, Adams wrote, they were temporarily stopped from entering by a "dapper [well dressed] lieutenant" who "did not know, until one of his private soldiers explained to him, who the United States were."

The Adamses were welcomed into Berlin diplomatic society, attending countless dinners and dances. Adams struck up friendly relations with King Frederick William III and other Prussian royalty and officials. He continued sending his observant reports home, and he negotiated a new treaty of friendship and trade with Prussia. Adams was also busy mastering German. He became so fluent in the language that he turned to translating German literature into English.

Although he had been a reluctant groom, Adams was a fond husband. Louisa and he wanted to start a family, but Louisa was troubled by miscarriages. Finally, after four miscarriages, Louisa became pregnant again in the fall of 1800. On April 12, 1801, she gave birth to a son, named George Washington Adams in honor of the first president.

John and Louisa's joy at the birth of their son was darkened by other events that came before it. John's brother Charles had suffered for some time from various illnesses. He may have had a mental illness as well as alcoholism. In December 1800, he died at the age of thirty-one. That same month, John Adams lost his bid for a second term as president. As of March 1801, the nation's third president was Thomas Jefferson.

Rather than give the Republican Jefferson the opportunity to fire his Federalist son, John Adams ended John Quincy's position as minister to Prussia himself before he left the presidency. By September 1801, John Quincy, Louisa, and George Adams were back in the United States.

CHAPTER SIX

POLITICS AND
ADVANCEMENT

I would fain [rather] be the man
of my whole country.

—John Quincy Adams, at the time he began
his political career, expressing his hope that he
could serve his entire nation rather than the
interests of one political party

At home in Massachusetts, Adams enjoyed a warm reunion with his parents. "At nine in the evening I reached my father's house at Quincy," he wrote in his diary on September 21, 1801. "Here I had the inexpressible delight of finding once more my parents, after an absence of seven years. . . . My parents received me with a welcome of the tenderest affection."

Louisa's experience was rather different. After first taking baby George to visit her parents, who were living in Washington, D.C., she traveled north to meet her husband's parents. "Had I stepped into Noah's Ark I do not think I could have been more utterly astonished," she wrote. Everything from the New Englanders' accents to their dinner hour to their church services seemed odd to her. She felt rejected by all of her husband's family—except by ex-President John Adams. "The old gentleman took a fancy to me," she wrote, "and he was the only one."

Adams set up a law office in Boston. In contrast to his earlier efforts to practice law, this time he had some success. Although he was not particularly happy with the life of a lawyer, he kept his spirits up by participating in a local science club that experimented with electricity, among other things. He also kept his hand in public affairs. Six months after returning to a solidly Federalist New England, Adams was elected on a Federalist Party ticket to the Massachusetts state senate.

As a state senator, Adams did not accomplish much. He was interested in improving the Massachusetts court system. He tried to fight bribery of elected officials. But he did not achieve either goal. Perhaps this contributed to his dissatisfaction with himself when he wrote in his diary in 1803, "I enter this day upon my thirty-seventh year with sorrow to think how long I have lived, and to how little purpose."

Given more time, Adams might have made a deeper imprint on state government. But he served less than a year in the state senate. In February 1803, the state legislature elected him to the U.S. Senate to replace a senator who was retiring.

SENATOR ADAMS

Before John and Louisa moved to Washington, D.C., their second child, whom they named John, was born. The baby's father—the new Senator Adams—was eager to get to the capital. President Jefferson had called the U.S. Senate into a special meeting to approve a new treaty with France that would finalize the Louisiana Purchase.

Under the treaty, the United States purchased the Louisiana territory of 830,000 square miles for $15 million, or three cents per acre. Members of Adams's own Federalist Party opposed the treaty, which would give the United States the land between the Mississippi River and Rocky Mountains. Adams was determined not to let party loyalties dictate his views. Instead, he sided with the republican President Jefferson. To Adams, the Louisiana Purchase was a way for the United States to gain global power and prestige. He wanted to cast his vote in favor of the treaty, which had to be approved by two-thirds of the Senate to become effective.

Though he tried mightily to hurry to Washington, Adams did not make it in time for the vote. Travel was slow. Louisa became ill. By the time the family reached the capital after twenty days of traveling, the Senate had already voted. None of the other Federalist senators voted in the treaty's favor. Although the Republican-led Senate ratified (passed) the treaty anyway, Adams wished he could have been there to represent the only Federalist voice in favor of doubling the size of the country.

FAMILY LIFE

Life in Washington, D.C., for the Adamses was busy. They lived less than three miles from the U.S. Capitol in a large house. Senator Adams usually began his day early, reading and writing until breakfast. He then walked to the Capitol, where the Senate started its sessions around noon. After a return walk home, he had dinner with his family at four in the afternoon. He played with his two sons and went

During the time the Adamses lived in Washington, D.C., the area was sparsely populated and consisted mainly of marshlands and rolling hills.

✧

horseback riding with Louisa. Supper was at nine, and bedtime was around eleven. John and Louisa also attended many parties. They dined with President Jefferson. Adams enjoyed playing chess with Secretary of State James Madison. He also took his Senate duties seriously and studied every law Congress had passed since 1789, as well as every decision of the U.S. Supreme Court.

Home life had its complications. Three-year-old George had something of a behavior problem. He could not be left alone without getting into mischief. He could not pay attention to anything for any length of time. Both John and Louisa worried about him. The boy's grandmother, however, liked him just as he was: "You must not look for an old head upon young shoulders," Abigail wrote. "A grave sedate [serious, quiet] Boy, will make a very... dull old man.... I ... am really rejoiced to hear that he is a wild Boy."

In 1805 Adams decided that his sons would be better off staying in Quincy instead of living in Washington. George, at four years old, went to live with an aunt and uncle. John, age two, stayed with Abigail Adams. Although Louisa was not happy about being separated from her children, she bowed to her husband's wishes. Two summers later, she gave birth to another son, Charles Francis Adams, named for Adams's dead brother Charles.

PARTY POLITICS

With his children taken care of, Senator Adams could concentrate on politics. The Senate—indeed, the entire country—was divided along party lines over how to best run the nation. Yet Adams distanced himself from both the Republican Party of President Jefferson and the opposition Federalist Party. He acted independently even though he owed his Senate seat to Massachusetts Federalists.

One of the issues creating bitter party division in the nation was international relations. Great Britain and France were at war with each other. Their conflict interfered with U.S. shipping on the Atlantic Ocean. The United States tried to keep a neutral policy and was repaid by both France and Britain with attacks on U.S. ships and seizures of ship cargoes. In a practice known as impressment, British navy captains also captured sailors from U.S. ships. The captains claimed the sailors were deserters from the British navy, even when the sailors had documents proving that they were U.S. citizens. Impressment became an emotional issue for many Americans.

When the British began their policy of impressment, many American-born seamen were unfairly arrested.

✧ ─────────────

In June 1807, a British warship, the *Leopard,* fired on a U.S. ship, the *Chesapeake,* off the coast of Virginia. The U.S. ship had refused to allow the British aboard to search for sailors to impress. Around twenty Americans died in the fight.

The *Chesapeake* affair created heated controversy in Washington, D.C., and in Senator Adams's life. Adams was outraged at Britain's attack. To protest the British action, he joined a rally attended almost entirely by Republican Party members. Other New England Federalists were unwilling to speak out against Great Britain. They knew that New England shipping and trading businesses relied on good relations with the European nation. These Federalists did not believe that the issues of cargo seizures and impressments were worth risking harm to that relationship.

The senator from Massachusetts also represented Federalist New England, but he insisted on following his own judgment. That judgment placed him more and more on the side of the Republican Party and of President Jefferson. Soon Jefferson proposed an embargo (ban) on all international shipping from U.S. ports. Adams supported and even helped write the law to carry it out. The resulting Embargo Act of 1807 barred U.S. exports leaving the United States on U.S. and foreign ships. The hope was that Great Britain and France, which benefited from U.S. trade, would be swayed to stop their attacks on U.S. ships.

In fact, the embargo did not change Britain and France's behavior for the better. And to Federalists, Adams's own behavior only got worse. In January 1808, he met with other Republicans in Congress to nominate Republican Secretary of State James Madison to run for president at the end of President Jefferson's second term in the fall.

Adams's actions were too much for the Federalist Massachusetts legislature to take. The legislature voted to replace Adams with a more reliable Federalist. Although he was entitled to remain in office until 1809, Adams resigned in June 1808. After that, he considered himself a member of the Republican Party.

ANOTHER VOYAGE

Adams and his family moved back to Boston, where the ex-senator practiced law once again. Two of his cases took him to the Supreme Court in Washington, D.C., in 1809. While in the capital, Adams attended the inauguration of the new president, James Madison, on March 4. That evening he went to an inaugural party, which he described in his diary: "The crowd was excessive—the heat oppressive, and the entertainment bad."

Two days later, while eating breakfast, Adams was interrupted with a messenger carrying a note from President Madison, asking Adams to call on him. At the meeting, Madison asked Adams to accept his nomination to become the U.S. minister to Russia. Adams accepted immediately. After some delay, the Senate approved the appointment in July.

John and Louisa decided that their two older boys, George and John, should stay behind with relatives. Two-year-old Charles Francis would travel with them. On August 5, they sailed from Charlestown, Massachusetts, on a journey of eighty days. They arrived in Russia on October 23, 1809.

CHAPTER SEVEN

MAN OF THE WORLD

I am forty-five years old. Two-thirds of a long life are past, and I have done nothing to distinguish it by usefulness to my country or to mankind.

—diary entry of John Quincy Adams on his birthday, July 11, 1812, by which time he had traveled through Europe, held office in both the Massachusetts and U.S. Senates, represented clients before the U.S. Supreme Court, and served as U.S. minister to three countries

For John Quincy Adams, his arrival in Russia in October 1809 was a return visit. He had been there twenty-eight years earlier, with Francis Dana. Back then the leader of Russia, Empress Catherine the Great, did not even recognize the United States as an independent nation. By 1809 the Russian Czar, Alexander I, not only recognized the United States of America but also embraced its new minister to Russia. Together, Adams and Alexander forged a strong relationship between their two nations.

Czar Alexander and Adams both enjoyed strolling about Saint Petersburg. Speaking in French, they discussed everything from the weather to international politics. The two men even discussed their habit of wearing flannel underwear.

Adams came to know other foreign diplomats in Saint Petersburg and spent much of his time exchanging information and sending home observations on world politics. As a couple, John and Louisa attended countless social affairs. During the long winter, a favorite outdoor pastime was sliding down icy hills at night with large groups of other adults.

Adams participated in the socializing but complained in his diary. "The night parties abroad seldom break up until four or five in the morning," he wrote. "It is a life of such irregularity and dissipation [wasteful amusement] as I cannot and will not continue to lead."

─────── ✧ ───────

Diplomatic social events often included dancing. Adams disliked the gatherings, which could last into the wee hours of the morning.

FITNESS NUT

The life of a diplomat in the 1800s involved plenty of socializing, and socializing involved a lot of heavy dinners. During his career, John Quincy Adams served as the U.S. minister to four countries—the Netherlands, Prussia, Russia, and Great Britain. That added up to countless hours sitting at a dining table.

To counteract all that sitting, eating, and drinking, Adams got into the habit of taking long walks. His approach to exercise was disciplined and regular. He dedicated a particular time of day to walking. He kept track of the length of his walks. A six-mile stroll was not unusual for him. For a time, while minister to Russia in the winter of 1811–1812, he arose at five in the morning, took a cold bath, read five chapters of the Bible in German, and then went on a six-mile walk—all before breakfast. (He soon abandoned the cold bath and got up a little later.)

Always interested in scientific measurements, Adams recorded the length of his typical stride, or walking step. It was two feet, six inches, "and eighty-eight one hundreds of an inch." He calculated that a mile took him 1,060 paces, but if the path was hilly or he had gravel in his shoe, the same distance required 1,120 paces.

Much as he enjoyed walking, he was also interested in other exercise. During his stay in Russia, while serving as minister, a French diplomat recommended tennis. The problem with tennis, as Adams wrote in his diary, was that "I do not understand it and think it too late to begin to learn."

As an alternative to walking, Adams took up swimming. While serving as secretary of state, he swam in Washington, D.C.'s Potomac River practically every day in the capital's long, hot summers. As with walking, he was systematic and disciplined about his swimming. He was always trying to improve on his performance. During the summer of 1822, Adams set a new record for himself by swimming for fifty minutes without having his feet touch the bottom. The following year, he increased this to eighty minutes. He did not try to improve on that, as his wife and doctor begged the fifty-six-year-old Adams to swim for one hour and then get out. He agreed but made a new contest for himself by swimming with his clothes on, which was much more difficult than swimming undressed.

As president, Adams kept on walking and swimming. His Potomac River swims brought him some adventures. One morning in June 1825, President Adams and an assistant rowed a rickety old boat into the water with the plan of crossing the river and swimming back to shore. The boat was so leaky, the men had to jump out in the middle of the river. With difficulty, they made it back to shore, but a passerby thought that the president had drowned. It was hours before Adams showed up at the Executive Mansion and assured Louisa Adams that he was not dead.

Despite such complaints, Adams continued to lead the socially active life of a nineteenth-century diplomat. He, Louisa, and Charles Francis settled into Saint Petersburg. In August 1811, a fourth Adams child, Louisa Catherine, was born.

PUBLIC AND PRIVATE TURMOIL

Adams had much to report back to President Madison in his role as a diplomatic observer. Europe was in turmoil. Under the leadership of Napoleon Bonaparte, France invaded Russia in the summer of 1812. The Russians fought back hard, forcing the French army to retreat in October 1812. At the same time, ongoing disagreements between the United States and Great Britain over such issues as impressments and interference with U.S. shipping erupted into the War of 1812.

———————————— ✧ ————————————

*On June 19, 1812, the United States declared war on Great Britain.
The battles of the War of 1812 took place at sea, on U.S. soil,
and in British Canada.*

The War of 1812 forced John and Louisa to postpone plans to bring their sons George and John to Russia. During the war, ocean travel was risky. Then, amid the upheaval on the international scene, John and Louisa Adams experienced a private tragedy. Their baby Louisa Catherine died on September 15, 1812, after a severe illness. Both parents grieved deeply. JQA wrote to Abigail Adams, "The wound of the heart still bleeds. It can never be entirely healed!"

Work distracted Adams from his sorrow somewhat. Shortly after his baby's death, he became engaged in trying to arrange peace talks with Great Britain. In early 1814, the British finally agreed to meet with U.S. negotiators in Sweden. President Madison appointed a peace commission of five prominent Americans, including John Quincy Adams, to hold talks with the British.

NEGOTIATING PEACE

In the spring of 1814, Adams left Louisa and Charles behind in Russia. After he reached Stockholm, Sweden's capital, he received a message informing him that the location of the talks had been changed to Ghent, Belgium. Adams reached this destination in June, and he and the other Americans got to work.

They also got to squabbling. Adams himself was a key source of tension within the group of Americans. He grew impatient with his fellow negotiators and criticized practically everything about them—much as he had criticized the students and professors at Harvard nearly thirty years before. He particularly objected to their practice of playing cards until four in the morning. "They sit after dinner," he wrote in his diary, "and drink bad wine and smoke cigars."

Despite the friction, the peace negotiations progressed. The British made clear that they would not move on the issue of impressments of sailors on U.S. ships. But the U.S. delegation decided to accept a peace treaty anyway. This went against President Madison's instructions, but the negotiators felt it was the only way toward peace. In fact, as JQA quickly concluded, peace would best be achieved by agreeing simply to roll back the clock to the situation before the War of 1812 began. Territory seized by each side would be given back to the other. Disputes over impressments, shipping, fishing rights, and boundaries would be left unsettled.

These were the terms to which the U.S. and British negotiators agreed in the Treaty of Ghent, signed December 24, 1814. They sent the treaty off to Washington, D.C., for acceptance by the president and ratification by

Evening Gazette Office,

Boston, Monday, 10, A.M.

The following most highly important handbill has just been issued from the CENTINEL press We deem it duty that we owe our Friends and the Public to assist in the prompt spread of the Glorious News.

Treaty of PEACE signed and arrived.

CENTINEL Office, Feb. 15, 1815, 8 o'clock in the morning.

WE have this instant received in Thirty-two hours from New-York the following

Great and Happy News!
FOR THE PUBLIC.

To BENJAMIN RUSSELL, Esq. Centinel Office, Boston.

New-York, Feb. 11, 1815—Saturday Evening, 10 o'clock.

SIR—

I HASTEN to acquaint you, for the information of the Public, of the arrival here this afternoon of H. Br. M. sloop of war Favorite, in which has come passenger Mr CARROLL, American Messenger, having in his possession

A Treaty of Peace

Between this Country and Great Britain, signed on the 26th December last. Mr Baker also is on board, as Agent for the British Government, the same who was formerly Charge des Affairs here.

Mr Carroll reached town at eight o'clock this evening. He shewed to a friend of mine, who is acquainted with him, the packquet containing the Treaty, and a London newspaper of the last date of December, announcing the signing of the Treaty.

It depends, however, as my friend observed, upon the act of the President to suspend hostilities on this side.

The gentlemen left London the 2d Jan. The Transit had sailed previously from a port on the Continent.

This city is in a perfect uproar of joy, shouts, illuminations, &c. &c. I have undertaken to send you this by Express—the rider engaging to deliver it by Eight o'clock on Monday morning. The expense will be 225 dollars.—If you can collect so much to indemnify me I will thank you to do so.

I am with respect, Sir, your obedient servant,

JONATHAN GOODHUE.

☞ We most heartily felicitate our Country on this auspicious news, which met he eched on as whstl/ sʰPubrot—Cᴇɴᴛɪɴᴇʟ.

PEACE EXTRA.

✧ ————

This poster announces the signing of the Treaty of Ghent in 1814, which ended the War of 1812. Adams played a key role in negotiating peace with Great Britain.

the Senate. On January 8, 1815, while the treaty was making its way across the ocean, U.S. General Andrew Jackson defeated the British in the Battle of New Orleans, the greatest U.S. victory of the War of 1812. Neither he nor anyone else in the United States knew that the war was supposed to be over until the treaty reached Washington in February 1815.

MINISTER TO ENGLAND

After completing negotiations at Ghent, Adams sent word to his wife in Saint Petersburg that she should close up their house there and meet him in Paris. He would not be returning to his duties as minister to Russia. Instead, as a reward for his service, President Madison was sending Adams to London to take the most important post a U.S. diplomat could hold: minister to Great Britain.

After months of separation, John, Louisa, and Charles Francis were reunited in Paris in late March of 1815. When they arrived together in London on May 25, they enjoyed another, larger reunion. Sons George, fourteen years old, and John, twelve, awaited them. The two boys had not seen their parents for more than five years.

Pleased as he was to have his family together, JQA was not altogether pleased with his older sons. Their study habits and intellectual achievements fell short of his high standards. He tried to put them on the type of schedule he had endured as a boy, with lessons in Latin, Greek, and French. George in particular worried his father. He frequently felt ill. He was not a good student, and he resisted his father's strict schedule.

Adams spent two years in London as U.S. minister to Britain. Adams thoroughly enjoyed the time he spent in the big, bustling city.

Despite worries over his older son, Adams enjoyed life in London. His duties as minister were not difficult. The Adamses attended many dinner parties, and Adams also spent much of his time writing poetry.

One of Adams's tasks while minister was to lessen the likelihood that military action could break out between the United States and Great Britain on the Great Lakes. The lakes formed part of the border between the United States and British Canada, and they were still teeming with warships left over from the War of 1812. Adams negotiated with British officials to greatly reduce warships and other arms on the Great Lakes. These talks resulted in an important treaty, the Rush-Bagot Agreement of 1817, signed for the United States by Richard Rush, who became minister to Britain after Adams. Under this agreement, the United States and Britain would maintain a peaceful border between them by reducing military forces around the Great Lakes to a bare minimum.

After two terms in office, Madison stepped down as president. His secretary of state, James Monroe, was elected to office in March of 1817. Monroe soon sent word to London of a new assignment for the U.S. minister. John Quincy Adams was to take Monroe's old job as secretary of state. This important cabinet position had been a stepping-stone to the presidency for Monroe, James Madison, and Thomas Jefferson. Adams's parents wrote to urge that he accept the job. As he had so many times in the past, Adams accepted his appointment.

Adams's extensive travels and fluency in many languages contributed to his success in international affairs. Many historians consider Adams our nation's most successful secretary of state.

CHAPTER EIGHT

SEASONED SECRETARY OF STATE

The Florida Treaty was the most important incident in my life, and the most successful negotiation ever consummated by the Government of this Union.

—John Quincy Adams, referring to the Transcontinental Treaty, which allowed the United States to obtain Florida and also gain recognition that U.S. territory extended to the Pacific Ocean

On August 16, 1817, John Quincy Adams stepped onto U.S. soil for the first time in eight years. The country had grown. It had nearly nine million residents, up from seven million in 1809. Towns and factories had sprung up, and trade was thriving.

Adams's family had experienced more sobering changes. His older sister Nabby was dead from breast cancer. His brother Thomas suffered from alcoholism.

Adams's professional life may have helped fill the emotional void created by his family's problems. People praised Adams as the successful statesman that he was. In September 1817, he and Louisa went to Washington, D.C., so that Adams could begin his duties as secretary of state. There Adams enjoyed a reputation as a knowledgeable negotiator, diplomat, and interpreter of world affairs.

The Adams children stayed in the Boston area to continue their education. In Washington, John and Louisa lived with Louisa's sister at first, before moving to a house of their own. The new secretary of state walked to work and continued his habit of taking long strolls. He also enjoyed swimming in the nearby Potomac River.

Adams was busy in his new position. He talked frequently with President Monroe about international affairs. He also corresponded with U.S. diplomats abroad, who reported to him, and he met with foreign diplomats in Washington. But the daily routine required of the secretary of state was only part of Adams's job. Among his most important concerns were the nation's boundaries and possible expansion of U.S. territory. He proved to be a creative and skilled secretary of state, finding opportunities for the nation to grow and formulating solutions to its diplomatic problems.

DRAWING NEW BOUNDARIES

Adams addressed tensions along the northwestern border with British Canada first, which was still an important issue for the United States. He oversaw negotiations that led to the Treaty of 1818. In this agreement, the United States and Britain drew the border between the United States and British Canada from Lake of the Woods (in the Minnesota Territory) west to the Rocky Mountains. The land west of the Rockies, known as Oregon Country, was left open to citizens of both countries. This provision created possibilities for future expansion of U.S. territory. The treaty also gave Americans fishing privileges in the rich waters off British Newfoundland and Labrador, northeast of Canada.

Adams's next project led to an even greater expansion of territory for the United States. President Monroe and Adams wanted to assert total U.S. control over Florida. Although Spain claimed the eastern half of the territory, many American settlers lived there. The goal to claim all of Florida for the United States became both more complicated and more achievable after General Andrew Jackson made a bold move in 1818. Jackson took the initiative to invade Florida. He drove out Spanish leaders, conquered the Spanish towns of Saint Marks and Pensacola, and destroyed Native American villages.

During General Andrew Jackson's campaign in Florida, U.S. troops destroyed Native American villages and took many Seminoles hostage.

Jackson defended his actions as necessary to stop attacks by the Seminoles and runaway slaves against U.S. citizens on the Georgia frontier. The Seminoles and other Native Americans had been squeezed out of their lands in Georgia. In response, they and the former slaves launched regular attacks on white settlers there. After these attacks, the Seminoles fled into Spanish Florida.

President Monroe had told Jackson to stop the raids. Jackson's invasion, however, risked a crisis in relations with Spain. Every member of Monroe's cabinet (advisors), except for one, wanted to give Spain back its land. That one cabinet member was Secretary of State Adams. Where others saw a giant crisis, he saw a great opportunity.

Adams met with Spain's minister to the United States, Luis de Onis y Gonzales. He said that Spain could have its Florida lands back just as soon as Spain could maintain control over them. But, as Adams pointed out, the Native American raids and Jackson's military invasions showed that Spain was not really in control. To maintain control and power in Florida, Spain needed to enlarge its own military forces there.

Adams knew that Spain was no longer rich or powerful enough to send more forces to Florida. So he proposed another solution to Onis: Spain should transfer Florida to the United States. Without a better alternative, Onis agreed. The two wrote the Adams-Onis, or Transcontinental, Treaty.

The United States obtained Florida for a price of only five million dollars. That was not all. Adams and Onis agreed on a clear western border between the U.S.-owned lands of the Louisiana Purchase and Texas, which was still a Spanish province. They further agreed on a line between the two nations' territories that ran from the Louisiana territory all the way to the Pacific Ocean. As part of the deal, Spain gave up all claims to land in the Oregon Territory, and the United States recognized Spanish ownership of Texas.

With a boundary line drawn to the Pacific, the territory of the United States extended across the entire continent. Adams had changed the shape and size of the nation. Some historians consider the Transcontinental Treaty the greatest diplomatic victory won by any individual in U.S. history.

CAPITAL LIFE

Government business was not all that claimed Adams's time. Washingtonians expected cabinet members and their wives to give and attend parties. At first, the Adamses disappointed their neighbors and politicians. They did not follow the tradition of visiting every new person of any importance who came to town. Some whispered that the Adamses were snobbish after years of socializing with European royalty. The Adamses were private and somewhat aloof by nature, but they were not intentionally out to snub the residents of the capital.

In response to the criticism, they went out of their way to be more social. Louisa hosted gatherings every Tuesday for fifty to one hundred visitors. She soon became one of the most popular hostesses in Washington. From time to time, the Adamses also threw large balls for hundreds of people.

Family life continued to be a trial for Adams. After the death of his mother, Abigail, in late 1818, Adams realized that his brother Thomas's life had fallen apart. Thomas drank to extreme excess and gambled. In visits to Quincy, Adams tried to convince Thomas to improve his habits and worked out an arrangement to support Thomas's children.

After being criticized for their private nature, the Adamses became more social. They often hosted receptions for prominent politicians and officials, such as the popular Andrew Jackson (above center).

———————————— ✧ ————————————

Adams's own sons troubled him greatly. George graduated from Harvard in 1821, but his performance was a disappointment. He turned to the study of law but was hindered by continuing physical and emotional health problems. The younger sons, John and Charles Francis, did so poorly in their studies at Harvard that when they asked to visit Washington for Christmas, Adams said no. When young John wrote a letter pleading to come, Adams responded, "I would feel nothing but sorrow and shame in your presence." In the spring of 1823, the college expelled John, along with a group of other students, for taking part in a riot.

A Weighty Assignment

Adams received one unusual assignment as secretary of state that appealed to his interest in science. Congress instructed him to research and write a report on the different ways the states and other nations regulated weights and measures. He was also to propose a uniform system of weights and measurements for the United States.

For Adams, this was a meaty project. He researched the history of weighing and measuring. He surveyed the practices of states and foreign nations. He even carried out his own experiments, weighing kernels of wheat and other grains.

Adams concluded that the metric system, as used in France, was the best in the world. He urged the United States to adopt it. His enthusiasm for the meter (3 feet) was almost manic. In the report that he published in 1822, he wrote that if "one language of weights and measures will be spoken from the equator to the poles," this would be a step toward "universal peace." There was more. Adoption of the metric system worldwide, he said, "would help cast down the Spirit of Evil."

Congress did not act on its fanatical reporter's recommendations. However, ever since, experts in weights and measures have admired the report as one of the best on the subject.

Adams (far left) *helped President Monroe* (standing) *and his cabinet members form the Monroe Doctrine, which became an important part of U.S. foreign policy.*

THE MONROE DOCTRINE

By late 1823, Adams had important State Department business to distract him from his troubles. New nations in South and Central America were declaring their independence from Spain. President Monroe formally recognized them as free countries, but Spain indicated that it might fight to win back these former colonies. The Spanish king had the backing of France and other members of a group of European leaders known as the Holy Alliance.

Great Britain opposed the Holy Alliance. Instead, it wanted to make a declaration jointly with the United States against Spain's suspected plan. When this proposal reached President Monroe, he considered it very carefully. For all its territory, the United States was not a powerful nation. Keeping Spain and the Holy Alliance out of the Western Hemisphere (the western half of the globe) would be a daunting, if not impossible, task for the United States alone. Teaming up with Great Britain, the world's greatest naval power, had much appeal. On the other hand, the United States would be very much the weaker partner in any combination with Britain. That position appealed to few Americans.

The question Great Britain posed was so significant that Monroe took it to former presidents James Madison and Thomas Jefferson. They were concerned about getting the United States entangled in European affairs. But they found the British invitation to stand together against the other powers too tempting to turn down. Madison and Jefferson both advised President Monroe to join with Great Britain.

In the cabinet, Monroe's advisers also took this position—except for one man. As he had in the debate over Florida, John Quincy Adams staked out an independent position. Like the others, Adams wanted to take a firm stand against the Holy Alliance. But Adams wanted the United States to act on its own, not in an unequal partnership with Great Britain.

Adams felt it was time the United States declared the entire Western Hemisphere off limits to all European nations. He believed that European powers should no longer be allowed to colonize or interfere in the affairs of the Americas. Adams was not only concerned about potential Spanish attacks. He was also worried about Russian claims to land along the northwestern coast of North America. It was time, he said, to send a message to the entire world.

Adams's arguments convinced the president and the rest of the cabinet. On December 2, 1823, President Monroe sent a message to Congress. In it, he announced that the United States would not tolerate European interference in the Western Hemisphere. New European colonies in the Americas were similarly unacceptable. In exchange, the United States would not interfere with existing European colonies and it would not meddle in the affairs of European countries.

The United States lacked the military power to back up these bold statements. Still, the announcement told the world that the United States had its own policies and values, separate from those of European nations. By the mid-1800s, the announcement became known as the Monroe Doctrine—but it owed much of its flavor to Secretary of State John Quincy Adams.

CHAPTER NINE

A DISAPPOINTING PRESIDENCY BEGINS

I well know that I never was and never shall be what is commonly termed a popular man.
—John Quincy Adams, on his limitations as a candidate

John Quincy Adams served as secretary of state for both of President James Monroe's two terms of office. During the second term, Adams held another, unofficial position: presidential candidate. From the moment Monroe was sworn in for his second four-year term in March 1821, ambitious politicians started scrambling to win the election of 1824.

Among the leading contenders was General Andrew Jackson of Tennessee, hero of the Battle of New Orleans. Speaker of the House Henry Clay of Kentucky was another formidable candidate. One of Adams's fellow members of the cabinet, Secretary of the Treasury William Crawford of Georgia, also wanted to become president.

William Crawford (left) *and Henry Clay* (right) *joined Adams and Jackson as presidential candidates in the historic 1824 election.*

Secretary of War John Calhoun of South Carolina started out running for president but soon lowered his sights to the vice presidency instead.

Then there was Adams. He wanted to be president too. He always said he hated politics. But his repeated involvement in politics and public life showed that he clearly found some pleasure or reward in holding public office. He had also shown himself to be a talented government official. But he detested asking people for votes. In those days, candidates did not campaign actively among ordinary citizens, but their managers and supporters did. While Jackson, Clay, and Crawford openly sought support from influential people, Adams shrank back.

All the presidential candidates belonged to the Republican Party, including Adams, who had broken from the old Federalist Party years earlier during his term in the U.S. Senate. A group of Republican U.S. congressmen nominated Crawford for president. Jackson, Clay, and Adams received nominations from their state legislatures.

Jackson—fondly called "Old Hickory" by his supporters, because he was supposed to be as tough as hickory wood—was the front-runner. For the first time in U.S. history, people in sixteen states were directly electing

---

◇

Adams's most formidable opponent in the 1824 election was war hero Andrew Jackson (below). Jackson was popular among ordinary citizens.

officials known as presidential electors. These presidential electors would vote in the Electoral College, the body that elects the president and vice president. (In six other states, the legislatures, not the people, chose the electors.) This was the first election, then, in which appealing to the general population mattered. Jackson was a master at appealing to ordinary citizens. The war hero was uneducated and had little government experience, but people loved him.

Adams could not have been more different. He wrote in his diary that he knew he was a man of cold, stern, and sometimes uninviting manners. In the sixteen states that had popu-

———————————— ✧ ————————————

In this cartoon of the 1824 presidential election, Adams and Crawford pull ahead of Jackson while Clay laments having to drop out of the race.

A FOOT-RACE

lar voting in the fall of 1824, Jackson won approximately 43 percent of the ballots. Adams received around 31 percent.

But these tallies did not decide who would be president. What mattered was the vote of the Electoral College. In early December, those results were counted. Jackson had the greatest number of electoral votes—ninety-nine. Adams won eighty-four, followed by Crawford. Clay won the fewest electoral votes.

Still the vote was not conclusive. Under the Constitution at that time, a candidate had to receive a majority of the Electoral College votes to win. Jackson fell short of this requirement. In such circumstances, the Constitution provided that the House of Representatives had to choose a president from among the top three candidates.

As the fourth vote getter, Henry Clay was dropped from the race in the House of Representatives. But he had considerable influence in directing the votes of his supporters in the House. A month before the House vote on the presidency, Clay and Adams had a meeting. What they discussed is unknown. What is known is that on February 9, 1825, the House of Representatives voted for Adams as the next president of the United States. Clay's supporters in several states switched their vote from him to Adams, following Clay's lead. With this and other support, John Quincy Adams was elected the sixth president of the United States. He beat Andrew Jackson, who had won more popular votes and more electoral votes.

Shortly after his election, Adams chose Clay to be secretary of state in his new administration. Supporters of Andrew Jackson went wild. They cried out against the "corrupt bargain" that brought Adams to power and put Clay in the State Department. Jackson said, "Clay voted for Adams and made him President and Adams made Clay secretary of state. Is this not proof . . . of the understanding and corrupt coalition [union] between them." Jackson immediately started planning his campaign against Adams for the presidential election of 1828.

Adams's diary sheds little light on whether he and Clay had actually made a bargain of any kind. Certainly Clay was qualified to be secretary of state. But Adams's appointment of Clay gave the appearance that the men had struck a deal—and this infected his presidency from its very first day.

OPPOSITION FROM THE START

Adams was inaugurated as president on March 4, 1825, with John Calhoun as vice president. In his inaugural speech, Adams referred to "the peculiar circumstances of the recent election." Under these circumstances, he knew he was "Less possessed of your [the public's] confidence" than any of the presidents who came before him. He promised that he possessed "a heart devoted to the welfare of our country."

But Adams's opponents in Congress, many of them supporters of Andrew Jackson, were not interested in his heart's devotion. They were more interested in spoiling his presidency. From the very beginning of his term of office, Adams could gather little support for his proposals. The new president wanted the federal government to build a large network of internal improvements (roads, canals, harbors, and similar projects). He also urged the establishment of a national university and a naval academy. Congress would not go along.

In his first annual message to Congress on December 5, 1825, Adams also proposed that the United States build an "astronomical observatory," a structure made for observing and studying the stars and planets. He wanted to appoint an official astronomer "to be in constant attendance of observation upon the phenomena of the heavens." European nations had more than one hundred of these "lighthouses of the skies," Adams observed. Similar progress by the United States should not be held back "by the will of our constituents," that is, by the desires of U.S. citizens.

People heaped ridicule and criticism on Adams for his lofty suggestion. The phrase "lighthouses of the skies" became a national joke. Opponents of Adams also pointed out the arrogance of a president who thought that the government had the power to build projects such as "astronomical observatories," despite the will of the people. John Quincy Adams's presidency was off to a disappointing start.

CHAPTER TEN

FROM BAD TO WORSE

I can scarcely conceive of a more harassing,
wearying, teasing condition of existence.

—John Quincy Adams, on life as president
of the United States

From a poor start, Adams's presidency only got worse.
Some of his problems stemmed from his refusal to play the
game of politics. As president, Adams had the right to
appoint people who were loyal to him to government posi-
tions. He did not. Government jobs continued to be held
by people who had held them in the past, including people
who wanted his presidency to fail.

Adams also hurt his political support by pursuing policies that angered southern leaders and voters. In Georgia,
for example, he disagreed with the governor's approach to
grabbing land from the Creek Indians. Adams was not a
great friend of Native Americans, but he knew they were
quickly losing their lands to the expanding United States.

He tried to craft a fairer deal for the Creek Indians. For his efforts, Adams received the hostility of Georgians and other southerners who wanted no obstacles in the path of taking over lands held by Native Americans.

Southerners also objected to Adams's proposal to send U.S. representatives to a meeting in Panama of new Latin American and Caribbean nations in 1826. The new nations had outlawed slavery. Some southerners feared that the meeting would call for the outlawing of slavery in all of the Western Hemisphere. Others did not want the U.S. representatives sitting down as equals with representatives from Caribbean island nations who were former slaves. Even after the Senate finally confirmed two U.S. delegates in the spring of 1826, the House of Representatives refused to approve the money to pay for their trip. Once the delegates finally set out for Panama, one of them died during the voyage, and the other arrived after the meeting was over.

The president again crossed southerners when he signed the Tariff of 1828. Adams favored increasing tariffs (fees charged on goods bought from foreign countries). The tariffs would make foreign products more expensive than U.S. products. That was good for U.S. companies in the North and West, which competed with European companies. But for the South, increased tariffs only meant higher prices for goods they needed to buy.

Southern anger served the interests of pro-Jackson politicians, who were delighted to whip up fury against President Adams. Southerners called the tariff law the "Tariff of Abominations." The tariff led Vice President John Calhoun to write a document in which he announced a "doctrine of nullification," the idea that any state had the right to disregard any federal law that trampled on its rights.

GLOOM AT THE TOP

Despite all the controversy and criticism of President Adams, the nation did not suffer during his term. Factories and farms were productive. Some internal improvements progressed. The Erie Canal started operations between Albany and Buffalo, New York, serving as a

————————————————— ✧ —————————————————

The Erie Canal reduced the cost of shipping goods and spurred the first great westward movement of settlers.

shipping route between the Atlantic Ocean and the Great Lakes. The government-funded National Road was extended from Cumberland, Maryland, to Zanesville, Ohio, opening a travel route from the eastern United States to the Midwest. Construction began on the Chesapeake and Ohio Canal, intended to link Washington, D.C., with points west. Workers also began building the Baltimore and Ohio Railroad, the first passenger railroad in the United States.

Still, the setbacks and ridicule took their toll on President Adams. For a time, he lost his appetite and became sickly. With no important victories or accomplishment to boost him, he found the daily routine of being president a chore.

Despite his gloom, Adams mostly kept to a regular schedule of rising by five in the morning and going for a swim or walk before breakfast. His days were usually occupied with paperwork and meetings. In the evenings, he often worked more, although he also enjoyed playing the game of billiards. The president grew interested in botany and liked to garden and conduct research into plant species.

Events in his family life did not improve Adams's spirits. His father, John Adams, died on July 4, 1826, causing him much sorrow. His oldest son, George, continued to be of great concern. George seemed to be an alcoholic, and he often behaved strangely. George's own fiancée broke off their engagement because of his problems and married his brother John. John was living with President and Mrs. Adams in Washington, D.C. John's daughter was the first baby born in the Executive Mansion, later known as the White House.

John Quincy Adams, Poet

Diplomat, senator, congressman, secretary of state, president—
John Quincy Adams engaged in all these careers, but the
career he yearned for the most remained beyond his reach. For
practically his entire life, Adams wished to be a writer,
particularly of poetry. He dreamed of a life spent filling up
notebooks, of publishing successes, of literary fame. That was
not the life he had.

And yet, if poetry was not his life's work, it was one of his
life's passions and pastimes. Adams's love affair with poetry
started during his teenage years, when he was in Russia for
the first time. As he could not find a suitable school or tutor,
he turned to books. He discovered the English poets, and he
was hooked.

Adams wrote poetry when he was unhappy, such as during
his time as a law student. He also wrote when he felt inspired
or happy. During a trip to the Prussian province of Silesia with
Louisa in 1800, he arose one morning at two to climb a
mountain peak. As he hiked down the mountain, he felt so
moved by the natural beauty around him that he sat down to
write a poem about it.

But it did not take a mountain to move Adams to verse.
He seemed inspired by the sheer fun of making up rhymes.
After successfully completing negotiations to end the War of
1812, Adams and others were entertained by the daughters of
some dinner companions. One of the girls sang several verses
honoring the American guests, which the company all enjoyed.

The next day, Adams could not get his work done. Poetry
was on his mind—couplets (pairs of verse), to be exact. As he
explained in his diary of January 5, 1815, "On rising this
morning, instead of diplomatic papers and letters . . . the fancy
struck me of answering the couplets yesterday sung by Mr.

Meulemeester's daughter. So farewell for this day all [serious] occupation. I could think of nothing but my couplets." Adams spent the day writing his couplets and delivering them to Mr. Meulemeester's daughter. Such was the power of poetry for this otherwise highly serious diplomat.

Much of Adams's poetry survives to this day. One example, entitled "A Winter's Day," described how he passed a typical day when he and Louisa were separated. In this case, Adams was staying in a relative's house while serving in the U.S. Senate in Washington, D.C., and Louisa was home in Massachusetts. The poem is fourteen verses long. The poet describes his work in one of the verses:

> Then forth I sally for the day,
> And, musing politics or rhyme,
> Take to the Capitol my way,
> To join in colloquy sublime.
> There with the fathers of the land
> I mix in sage deliberation,
> And lend my feeble voice and hand
> With equal laws to bless the nation.

One of the ways candidates spread the word about their run for the presidency in 1828 was by printing their names or likenesses on copper coins and medals.

NOT A CHANCE

Adams never had a chance at winning a second term as president. Halfway through Adams's term, supporters of Jackson, William Crawford, and John Calhoun formed the Democratic Party. Its members were dedicated to limiting the federal government, defeating Adams in 1828, and electing Jackson. Adams's supporters—and those who favored a powerful federal government—became known as National Republicans.

The presidential campaign of 1828 was extremely personal. Both sides in the campaign launched attacks on the character and lives of the two candidates. Some accusations were downright ugly. Jackson's people said Adams had spent his time as a diplomat in Russia supplying the czar with young American women. Adams's supporters argued that Jackson and his wife of almost forty years were living in sin because her divorce to her first husband was not final when she married Jackson.

The campaigns also used positive messages to get the attention of voters. For the first time in U.S. history, the candidates' supporters distributed trinkets such as buttons, mugs, and bottles promoting their man. Jackson had the upper hand in this strategy, with his war hero status and down-to-earth frontiersman image.

State voting laws had changed to allow a greater number of people to vote. More than twice as many voters participated in the election of 1828 as had in 1824—and more than half of them voted for Andrew Jackson. In the Electoral College, Jackson received 178 electoral votes, to Adams's 83. Americans elected Andrew Jackson as their seventh president by a landslide.

John Quincy Adams was the first person to follow his own father into the highest office in the land. His father was the first U.S. president to lose a bid for a second term—and John Quincy Adams became the second. "The sun of my political life set in the deepest gloom," he wrote in his diary. For Adams, his life in public service seemed over.

Adams, pictured here in an 1845 daguerreotype, is the first president of whom there is any known photograph. Daguerreotypes, which are images on silver-plated paper, were the first popular form of photography.

CHAPTER ELEVEN

OLD MAN ELOQUENT

He must be demented [insane].

—Andrew Jackson, on Congressman John Quincy
Adams's fight to allow debate on slavery in
the House of Representatives

Losing his bid for a second term as president was a sharp blow to John Quincy Adams. But he and Louisa soon suffered a loss that cut far deeper. Their son George had remained troubled, drawn to drinking and gambling. He had hinted at suicide. On board a steamboat at the end of April 1829, George disappeared. One month later, his body was found in Long Island Sound. George Washington Adams was twenty-eight years old at the time of his death.

Both parents were grief stricken. People noticed that John Quincy Adams, at age sixty-two, looked old. He and Louisa were cheered by the marriage of their youngest son, Charles, in September 1829. But the pain of George's death was made even worse by concerns about their middle son John, who also was an alcoholic.

A NEW CAREER

Back in Quincy in the summer of 1830, Adams felt despondent. His public life seemed a failure. His private life was racked with tragedy.

Then, in September, influential citizens of Boston and Quincy asked Adams whether he would run for the House of Representatives. The former president responded that he had no desire to be elected and would not seek the office. But he promised he would serve if elected. In November 1830, voters did elect him over two other candidates. Adams wrote in his diary, "No election or appointment conferred upon [awarded to] me ever gave me so much pleasure."

Congressman John Quincy Adams's term of office began a year after his election, in December 1831. Louisa was reluctant to return to Washington. Still, she accompanied her husband, knowing that being involved in the nation's affairs had become as necessary to him as food and drink.

Serving in Congress gave Adams a purpose after the twin losses of the presidency and his son George. But it could not stop him from experiencing still more losses. His brother Thomas died in March 1832 of alcoholism. Two years later, the Adamses's middle son, John, died at the age of thirty-one. His fatal illness, too, was alcoholism. Of their four children, only one, Charles Francis, survived.

Adams grieved the losses of his brother and his son deeply. From his many losses and disappointments, however, he had learned how to carry on. He enjoyed his grandchildren—one girl from John and eventually seven

*Adams delighted in planting trees at his home in Quincy,
which became a National Historic Site in 1946.*

———————————————— ✧ ————————————————

children from Charles. He played games with them and
bought them toys and books. As he had since boyhood,
Adams still liked to talk with knowledgeable people for
hours about nearly everything. And when at his boyhood
home in Quincy, he labored for hours in his fields, planting trees, which had become a passion.

THE GAG RULE

Beginning in 1836, Adams's energies were occupied with
another passion: outlawing slavery. Slavery was legal in
southern states but illegal in northern states. It had become
one of the most controversial and divisive issues in
Congress. An antislavery movement had organized and
become vocal. Some people, called abolitionists, wanted to

end, or abolish, slavery immediately. Others wanted to prevent it from spreading into the nation's western territories. Whatever their exact opinion, opponents of slavery wrote petitions explaining their demands and sent them to Congress for consideration.

By the mid-1830s, Congress was receiving so many antislavery petitions that most were simply set aside and ignored. This did not stop the tide of antislavery petitions from rising even more. In response, Congress adopted the gag rule, which formally announced that citizen petitions on the subject of slavery would be disregarded.

Adams opposed the expansion of slavery into the territories, but he had never been an activist in the antislavery movement. But Congress's gag rule spurred him to action. The idea that the U.S. government would refuse to hear its citizens' petitions was unacceptable to him. The right to free speech—and the freedom of citizens to petition their government—were founding principles of the American republic. These principles had been written into the Constitution's First Amendment. Adams was also disgusted by what he viewed as the immoral and two-faced arguments of slaveholders. These southerners claimed that slavery was not only good for the southern economy but also good for slaves.

Adams took every opportunity to challenge the gag rule. Repeatedly, he rose from his seat in the House of Representatives to attempt to read antislavery petitions that violated the rule. Other congressmen called out, "Order, order!" to silence him. Adams did not care. Instead, he seemed to feed on their outrage. He shouted at, scolded, and taunted southern politicians.

Every two years, the citizens of Quincy reelected Adams to Congress, and at the start of every congressional session, he made impassioned speeches to repeal the gag rule. Presidents came and went—Andrew Jackson, Martin Van Buren, William Henry Harrison, John Tyler—all sidestepping the slavery question for fear of breaking apart the nation. But John Quincy Adams returned to Washington year after year to denounce southern slaveholders and their gag rule. To southerners, Adams was the Massachusetts Madman. To many northerners, he was a hero, "Old Man Eloquent."

———————————— ✧ ————————————

This satire on the enforcement of the gag rule depicts Adams's frustration in trying to present antislavery petitions to the House of Representatives. Adams lies atop a pile of petitions while a defender of slavery yells at him from behind a barrel, two slaves crouched by his side.

THE AMISTAD CASE

In 1839 a Spanish slave ship, the *Amistad,* was carrying captured Africans to a plantation in Cuba, where they were to be sold as slaves. While the ship was off the Cuban coast, a group of the captives mutinied, or rebelled, against their Spanish captors. The Africans killed the captain and much of the crew. They told the surviving crew members to take the ship back to Africa. Instead, the Spanish sailors tricked them and brought the *Amistad* to waters off Long Island, New York, where a U.S. warship captured it.

Spanish officials demanded that the United States return the ship, as well as its human cargo, to its Spanish owners. They argued that the Africans were slaves and the property of Spanish citizens. Two U.S. courts disagreed, ruling that the Africans were free men who had never been enslaved.

To please pro-slavery voters, the administration of President Martin Van Buren took the case to the U.S. Supreme Court. The administration argued that it was obliged by treaty to protect the property of Spanish citizens and that both countries recognized slaves as property.

Outraged at Van Buren's actions, ex-President John Quincy Adams offered to help the Africans' legal team. He joined the lawyer who had worked on the case in the lower federal courts. Both men presented arguments before the Supreme Court, which heard the case starting in February 1841. Lawyers for the Van Buren administration also argued their side of the case.

For four hours on February 24 and another four and one-half hours on March 1, Adams stood before the justices of the Supreme Court and spoke. He began by emphasizing that he represented people, not property. "I appear here on the behalf of thirty-six individuals," he began, "the life and liberty of every one of whom depend on the decision of this Court." Adams criticized and ridiculed the arguments of the Spanish government and of his own government, which asserted that the laws and treaties governing property applied to the Africans.

At the close of his argument, Adams pointed to a copy of the Declaration of Independence that hung on the wall before the Supreme Court justices. "That DECLARATION says that every man is 'endowed by his Creator with certain inalienable [guaranteed] rights,' and that among these are life, liberty, and the pursuit of happiness," he reminded his listeners. "The moment you come, to the Declaration of Independence, that every man has a right to life and liberty, an inalienable right, this case is decided. I ask nothing more in behalf of these unfortunate men, than this Declaration."

In March 1841, the Supreme Court issued its decision in the *Amistad* case. The court ruled that the federal government had no right to get involved in the case. The decision also concluded that the Africans were not slaves, but rather they had been captured in violation of international law banning the slave trade. They were freed and went to Sierra Leone, a British colony on the west coast of Africa. In appreciation, the leaders (Cinque, Kinna, and Kale) of the Africans gave Adams a Bible that he described as "splendidly bound" and signed by "Cinque, Kinna and Kale for the . . . Africans of the Amistad."

In January 1842, Adams beat back a resolution introduced by other congressmen to censure, or punish, him for repeatedly trying to discuss slavery in the House in violation of the gag rule. In fighting the censure resolution, he spoke out against slavery at the same time. His personal triumph soon led to a larger victory. On December 3, 1844, Congress repealed the gag rule. "Blessed, forever blessed, be the name of God," Adams wrote in his diary.

MORE FIGHTING

The slavery controversy took a toll on his health, but Adams had energy for other battles going on at the same time. In 1835 James Smithson, a British scientist, had given $500,000 to the United States in his will for creation of an institution to advance knowledge. Adams became the chairman of various committees to set up the institution, and he made sure the money was not spent on other matters. Some congressmen tried to pry the money away for their own pet projects, but Adams held firm. As president, he had earned scorn for suggesting that the government should support scientific and other pursuits of knowledge. Adams finally saw his opportunity. After much planning, Congress used Smithson's gift to create the Smithsonian Institution, a national museum and research center.

Adams had another opportunity to jump into the fray in 1836. That year Texas broke away from Mexico (which itself had become independent from Spain) and sought to join the United States as a slave territory. To Adams, Texas was simply part of the immoral slaveholding southern states. As usual, he was not gentle in his approach. "Are you not large and unwieldy enough already?" he asked sarcastically in a speech addressing pro-Texas congressmen. "Have you not Indians enough to expel [remove] from the land of their fathers' sepulchers [sacred burial sites], and to exterminate?" But Adams's opposition was not enough to prevent the admission of Texas as a slave state in 1845.

The following year, President James Polk asked Congress to declare war on Mexico. Polk and his supporters wanted to define the Texas border as well as take over the entire northern part of Mexico. This land would become the southwest region of the United States. Adams did not want to add more land to the slaveholding part of the United States. The seventy-nine-year-old congressman from Quincy opposed the war with all his might, but he had little strength left. In May 1846, Congress approved Polk's war in a vote that was punctuated by cries of "no!" from John Quincy Adams.

Adams grew weaker and weaker. He suffered a stroke in November 1846 but insisted on returning to Congress in February 1847. He spent the following summer and fall in Quincy, where he celebrated his eightieth birthday. Then he returned to Washington in December for yet another session of Congress. He was visibly ill, with shaking hands and a voice often too feeble to be heard.

On February 21, 1848, the House voted on a resolution to honor soldiers in recent battles of the Mexican War. Adams voted "no" on the resolution and started to his feet to say more. Before he could fully stand, he began to fall. Someone managed to catch him and prevent him from hitting the floor, and he was taken to the office of the Speaker of the House. He stayed in the Capitol for two days, asking to see Henry Clay, who came to Adams's side to say goodbye. When Louisa came to see him, he did not recognize her.

Surrounded by congressmen, John Quincy Adams breathed his last in the Capitol Building after suffering a stroke on the House floor.

John Quincy Adams died the evening of February 23, 1848, in the Capitol Building. Those who surrounded him as he lay dying heard him say one last sentence. Some reported that Adams said, "This is the end of earth, but I am content." Others heard him say, "This is the last of earth—I am composed."

LEGACY

During his lifetime, John Quincy Adams achieved and experienced a great deal. His far-flung travels alone, particularly as a younger person, distinguished him among the men of his time. Some historians rank him as the most outstanding diplomat and secretary of state in U.S. history. The

Transcontinental Treaty and Monroe Doctrine defined how the nation would grow into a great new power and how it would deal with the European powers. As a congressman, Adams forced the nation to confront the reality of its division into two parts, one slaveholding and the other free.

Adams's presidency was the weakest link in his long career. But four years out of eighty do not sum up the man. Adams, who so often wanted only to be left to his books and notebooks, gave his entire life to serve his country. To identify John Quincy Adams as the sixth president is true—but not enough. He was a public servant of the first order.

TIMELINE

1767 John Quincy Adams is born on July 11 in Braintree (later called Quincy), Massachusetts.

1775 The American Revolution begins.

1776 The United States declares its independence from Great Britain. Adams's father, John Adams, signs the Declaration of Independence.

1778 Adams travels with his father by ship from Massachusetts to France.

1779 Adams and his father return to the United States during the summer.

1780 The Adamses sail to France in February and then move to Amsterdam, the Netherlands, where Adams attends the University of Leyden.

1781 Fourteen-year-old Adams accompanies Francis Dana to Russia.

1783 After touring through northern Europe, Adams returns to Amsterdam and is reunited with his father. He helps his father prepare the papers for the Treaty of Paris, signed by Great Britain and the United States.

1785 After seven years in Europe, Adams returns to the United States.

1786 In the spring, Adams enrolls in Harvard College in Cambridge, Massachusetts.

1787 After graduating from Harvard, Adams begins a legal apprenticeship with Massachusetts lawyer Theophilus Parsons.

1790 Adams opens his own law office in Boston but has trouble starting his practice.

1794	Adams is appointed by President George Washington to be the U.S. minister to the Netherlands. He arrives in the Netherlands in October to begin his new duties.
1797	Adams marries Louisa Catherine Johnson in July. In October they go to Berlin, where Adams is the new U.S. minister to Prussia.
1801	Adams leaves Europe and moves back to Massachusetts.
1802	Adams is elected to the Massachusetts state senate.
1803	The Massachusetts legislature elects Adams to the U.S. Senate as a Federalist Party member.
1808	Adams switches his political party affiliation to the Republican Party. In June, Adams resigns his Senate seat so the Massachusetts legislature can replace him with a Federalist.
1809	President James Madison, a Republican, appoints Adams minister to Russia.
1812	The War of 1812 between the United States and Great Britain begins.
1814	Adams is appointed a peace commissioner to negotiate an end to the war with Great Britain. A peace treaty is signed in December.
1815	President Madison names Adams U.S. minister to Great Britain.
1817	James Monroe takes office as president and appoints Adams his secretary of state.
1818	Adams is responsible for the Treaty of 1818, which establishes a border between the United States and British Canada.

1819 Adams negotiates the Adams-Onis Treaty, also called the Transcontinental Treaty, under which Spain gives up claims to Florida and the Oregon Territory and agrees to a boundary between Spanish Texas and the Louisiana Territory.

1823 Adams helps formulate the Monroe Doctrine, in which the United States announces that it will no longer permit European interference with, or additional colonization of, the Western Hemisphere.

1824 In an election so close it must be decided by a special vote of the House of Representatives, Adams is elected president.

1828 Adams loses his bid to be reelected president to General Andrew Jackson.

1830 The people of Quincy elect former president Adams to the U.S. House of Representatives. He begins his term in December 1831.

1836 Adams begins his battle against the gag rule, which barred debate about slavery in the House of Representatives.

1841 Adams argues the *Amistad* case before the U.S. Supreme Court, defending the right of captured Africans to be freed.

1842 Adams beats back an attempt by southern congressmen to censure him for his fight against the gag rule.

1844 The House of Representatives repeals its gag rule.

1845 Over Adams's objection, the United States acquires slave-holding Texas, which becomes the twentieth-eighth state.

1848 Rising to speak in the House of Representatives, Adams collapses on February 21. He dies two days later.

SOURCE NOTES

7 John Quincy Adams, diary entry, 29 March, 1841. Quoted in "Adams Papers, Selected Manuscripts," *The Massachusetts Historical Society,* 2004, <http://www.masshist.org/adams_editorial> (March 17, 2004).

8 *Congressional Globe,* 27th Cong., 2d sess., 1842, 168, pt. 11. Quoted in "A Century of Lawmaking for a New Nation: U.S. Congressional Documents and Debates," Library of Congress, 2003, <http://memory.loc.gov/ammem/amlaw/lawhome.html> (March 17, 2004).

8 Ibid.

9 Robert V. Remini, *John Quincy Adams* (New York: Times Books, 2002), 150.

9 Ibid.

10 Charles Francis Adams, ed., *Memoirs of John Quincy Adams* (1874–1877; repr., Freeport, NY, Books for Libraries Press, 1969), vol. 1:7–8.

10–11 Lynne Withey, *Dearest Friend: A Life of Abigail Adams* (New York: Touchstone, 2002), 31.

11 Paul C. Nagel, *John Quincy Adams: A Public Life, A Private Life* (Cambridge, MA: Harvard University Press, 1997), 10.

12 John Quincy Adams to John Adams, letter, October 13, 1774. Quoted in "John Quincy Adams: One President's Adolescence," *The Massachusetts Historical Society,* 2004, <http://www.masshist.org/exhibitions/jqa.cfm> (March 17, 2004).

15 Withey, 61.

15 Charles Francis Adams, 1:7–8.

15 John Adams to John Quincy Adams, letter, August 11, 1777. Quoted in "John Quincy Adams: One President's Adolescence," *The Massachusetts Historical Society,* 2004, <http://www.masshist.org/exhibitions/jqa.cfm> (March 17, 2004).

16 Nagel, 12.

17 David McCullough, *John Adams* (New York: Simon & Schuster, 2001), 229.

18 John Adams, diary entry, February 21–23, 1778. Quoted in "John Quincy Adams: One President's Adolescence," *The Massachusetts Historical Society,* 2004, <http://www.masshist.org/exhibitions/jqa.cfm> (March 17, 2004).

19 John Adams, diary entry, February 24–26, 1778. Quoted in "John Quincy Adams: One President's Adolescence," *The Massachusetts Historical Society,* 2004, <http://www.masshist.org/exhibitions/jqa.cfm> (March 17, 2004).

21 Nagel, 17–18.

22 Abigail Adams to John Quincy Adams, letter, January 19, 1780. Quoted in "John Quincy Adams: One President's Adolescence," *The Massachusetts Historical Society,* 2004, <http://www.masshist.org/exhibitions/jqa.cfm> (March 17, 2004).

22 John Quincy Adams to John Adams, letter, March 16, 1780. Quoted in "John Quincy Adams: One President's Adolescence," *The Massachusetts Historical Society,* 2004, <http://www.masshist.org/exhibitions/jqa.cfm> (March 17, 2004).

22 John Adams to John Quincy Adams, letter, March 17, 1780. Quoted in "John Quincy Adams: One President's

Adolescence," *The Massachusetts Historical Society*, 2004, <http ://www.masshist.org/exhibitions /jqa.cfm> (March 17, 2004).

25 Francis Russell, *Adams, An American Dynasty* (New York: Ibooks, 1976), 149.

26 Nagel, 26.

26 John Quincy Adams to John Adams, letter, September 1, 1781. Quoted in "John Quincy Adams: One President's Adolescence," *The Massachusetts Historical Society*, 2004, <http ://www.masshist.org/exhibitions /jqa.cfm> (March 17, 2004).

26–27 Remini, 12.

28 Ibid., 15.

29 Russell, 149.

29 Richard Brookhiser, *America's First Dynasty: The Adamses, 1735–1918* (New York: The Free Press, 2002), 64.

30 Abigail Adams to John Quincy Adams, letter, March 2, 1780, "John Quincy Adams: One President's Adolescence," *The Massachusetts Historical Society*, 2004, <http://www.masshist.org/ exhibitions/jqa.cfm> (March 17, 2004).

30 Remini, 10.

30 Ibid., 37.

31 Charles Francis Adams, 1:21.

32 Nagel, 60–61.

33 Ibid., 45–46.

34 McCullough, 365.

35 Nagel, 57.

36 Ibid., 71.

38 Charles Francis Adams, 1:32.

40 Ibid., 1:193.

44 Brookhiser, 66.

46 Nagel, 132.

46 Charles Francis Adams, 1:247.

46–47 Russell, 166.

47 Withey, 285.

47 Nagel, 140.

49–50 Withey, 291.

52 Charles Francis Adams, 1:544.

54 Ibid., 2:387.

55 Ibid., 2:73.

56 Brookhiser, 66.

56 Nagel, 201.

59 Ibid., 209.

59 Ibid., 218.

65 Remini, 56.

70 Nagel, 279.

71 Ibid., 265.

75 Remini, 64.

80 Ibid., 74.

80 John Quincy Adams, "Inaugural Address of President John Quincy Adams, March 4, 1825," *The University of Oklahoma Law Center*, 2004, <http://www.law .ou.edu/hist/jqadams.html> (March 17, 2004).

81 Remini, 79–80.

82 Marie B. Hecht, *John Quincy Adams: A Personal History of an Independent Man* (New York: Macmillan Company, 1972), 452.

86–87 Charles Francis Adams, 3:138.

87 Ibid., 1:455–457.

89 Miller Center of Public Affairs, University of Virginia, "John Quincy Adams," *The American President*, 2003, <http://www. americanpresident.org> (March 17, 2004).

91 Remini, 141.

92 Nagel, 336.

94 Remini, 140.

96–97 John Quincy Adams, "Argument of John Quincy Adams Before the Supreme Court of the United States in the case of the United States, Appellants, vs. Cinque, and others, Africans, captured in the schooner Amistad, by Lieut. Gedney, Delivered on the 24th of February and 1st of March 1841," *History Central*, 2000, <http ://www.historycentral.com/amistad /amistad.html> (March 17, 2004).

97 Ibid.

97 Remini, 149.

98 Ibid., 152.

98–99 Ibid., 142.

100 Nagel, 414.

SELECTED BIBLIOGRAPHY

Adams, Charles Francis, ed. *Memoirs of John Quincy Adams.* 12 vols. 1874–77, Reprint. Freeport, NY: Books for Libraries Press, 1969.

Adams, John Quincy. "Argument of John Quincy Adams Before the Supreme Court of the United States in the case of the United States, Appellants, vs. Cinque, and others, Africans, captured in the schooner Amistad, by Lieut. Gedney, Delivered on the 24th of February and 1st of March 1841." *History Central,* 2000. <http://www.historycentral.com/amistad/amistad.html> (March 2004).

———. "Inaugural Address of President John Quincy Adams, March 4, 1825." *The University of Oklahoma Law Center,* 2004. <http://www.law.ou.edu/hist/jqadams.html> (March 2004).

Bemis, Samuel Flagg. *John Quincy Adams and the Foundations of American Foreign Policy.* New York: Alfred A. Knopf, 1969.

Brookhiser, Richard. *America's First Dynasty: The Adamses, 1735–1918.* New York: The Free Press, 2002.

Hargreaves, Mary W. M. *The Presidency of John Quincy Adams.* Lawrence: University Press of Kansas, 1985.

Hecht, Marie B. *John Quincy Adams: A Personal History of an Independent Man.* New York: Macmillan Company, 1972.

Howe, Charles A. "John Quincy Adams." *Dictionary of Unitarian and Universalist Biography,* 2000. <http: www.uua.org> (March 2004).

Hunt, James B. "Travel Experience in the Formation of Leadership," *Journal of Leadership Studies,* Winter 2000, 1992.

"John Quincy Adams: One President's Adolescence." *The Massachusetts Historical Society,* 2004. <http://www.masshist.org/exhibitions/jqa.cfm> (March 2004).

Kennan, George F. "On American Principles," *Foreign Affairs,* March–April 1995, 116.

McCullough, David. *John Adams.* New York: Simon & Schuster, 2001.

Nagel, Paul C. *John Quincy Adams: A Public Life, A Private Life.* Cambridge, MA: Harvard University Press, 1997.

Remini, Robert V. *John Quincy Adams.* New York: Times Books, 2002.

Russell, Francis. *Adams, An American Dynasty.* New York: Ibooks, 1976.

Shepherd, Jack. *The Adams Chronicles: Four Generations of Greatness.* Boston: Little Brown & Co., 1975.

Withey, Lynne. *Dearest Friend: A Life of Abigail Adams.* New York: Touchstone, 2002.

FURTHER READING AND WEBSITES

"Adams National Historic Park." *U.S. National Park Service.* <http://www.nps.gov/adam>. A travel guide to the fourteen-acre park and birthplace of John Quincy Adams, this site lists historic features as well as upcoming scheduled activities.

"The Adams Papers." *The Massachusetts Historical Society.* <http://www.masshist.org/adams_editorial/>. This collection contains family letters, diaries, and manuscripts from several generations of the Adams family, including letters and writings of John Quincy Adams. The website includes selected documents, timelines, and quotations.

Behrman, Carol H. *Andrew Jackson.* Minneapolis: Lerner Publications Company, 2003.

———. *John Adams.* Minneapolis: Lerner Publications Company, 2004.

Beschloss, Michael, ed. *American Heritage Illustrated History of the Presidents.* New York: Crown Publishers, 2000.

Bohannon, Lisa Frederiksen. *The American Revolution.* Minneapolis: Lerner Publications Company, 2004.

Childress, Diana. *The War of 1812.* Minneapolis: Lerner Publications Company, 2004.

Ferris, Jeri Chase. *Remember the Ladies: A Story about Abigail Adams.* Minneapolis: Carolrhoda Books, Inc., 2001.

Kroll, Steven. *John Quincy Adams: Letters from a Southern Planter's Son.* New York: Winslow Press, 2001.

Levy, Debbie. *James Monroe.* Minneapolis: Lerner Publications Company, 2005.

Miller Center for Public Affairs, University of Virginia. "John Quincy Adams." *The American President.* <http:// www. americanpresident.org.>. This detailed website covers Adams's entire life and includes links to other sites of interest.

Nardo, Don. *Thomas Jefferson.* New York: Children's Press, 2003.

Roberts, Jeremy. *James Madison.* Minneapolis: Lerner Publications Company, 2004.

Warrick, Karen Clemens. *War of 1812: "We Have Met the Enemy and They Are Ours."* Springfield, NJ: Enslow Publishers, 2002.

INDEX

About the Author

Debbie Levy earned a bachelor's degree in government and foreign affairs from the University of Virginia, as well as a law degree and master's degree in world politics from the University of Michigan. She practiced law with a large Washington, D.C., law firm and worked as a newspaper editor. Her previous books include *Lyndon B. Johnson*, *James Monroe*, and *The Vietnam War*. Levy enjoys paddling around in kayaks and canoes and fishing in the Chesapeake Bay region. She lives with her husband and their two sons in Maryland.
